African Women
Writing Diaspora

African Women Writing Diaspora

Transnational Perspectives in the Twenty-First Century

Edited by
Rose A. Sackeyfio

LEXINGTON BOOKS
Lanham • Boulder • New York • London

Published by Lexington Books
An imprint of The Rowman & Littlefield Publishing Group, Inc.
4501 Forbes Boulevard, Suite 200, Lanham, Maryland 20706
www.rowman.com

6 Tinworth Street, London SE11 5AL, United Kingdom

Copyright © 2021 The Rowman & Littlefield Publishing Group, Inc.

All rights reserved. No part of this book may be reproduced in any form or by any electronic or mechanical means, including information storage and retrieval systems, without written permission from the publisher, except by a reviewer who may quote passages in a review.

British Library Cataloguing in Publication Information Available

Library of Congress Cataloging-in-Publication Data

Names: Sackeyfio, Rose A., editor.
Title: African women writing diaspora : transnational perspectives in the twenty-first century / edited by Rose A. Sackeyfio.
Description: Lanham : Lexington Books, [2021] | Includes bibliographical references and index. | Summary: "African Women Writing Diaspora examines the works of contemporary African female writers through diaspora perspectives on the constructions of identity in transnational spaces. This collection interrogates the ways in which women construct new ways of telling the African story in the global age of social, economic, and political transformation"— Provided by publisher.
Identifiers: LCCN 2021007204 (print) | LCCN 2021007205 (ebook) | ISBN 9781793642431 (cloth) | ISBN 9781793642455 (paperback) | ISBN 9781793642448 (epub)
Subjects: LCSH: African literature—21st century—History and criticism. | African literature—Women authors—History and criticism. | African diaspora in literature. | Women, Black, in literature. | Identity (Philosophical concept) in literature.
Classification: LCC PL8010 .A3546 2021 (print) | LCC PL8010 (ebook) | DDC 809/.89287096—dc23
LC record available at https://lccn.loc.gov/2021007204
LC ebook record available at https://lccn.loc.gov/2021007205

Dedication
This book is dedicated to my Mother, Dorothy Wright, whose life inspired my journey of self-discovery that is still unfolding

Contents

Introduction   1
Rose A. Sackeyfio

1   Memory, Identity, and Return in Yaa Gyasi's *Homegoing*   15
     Rose A. Sackeyfio

2   Malian Immigration in France: Perspectives from African Women Writers of French Expression   29
     Cheryl Toman

3   Waithood and Girlhood in NoViolet Bulawayo's *We Need New Names*   45
     Amanda Lagji

4   Sexuality, Resilience, and Mobility in Amma Darko's *Beyond the Horizon* and Chika Unigwe's *On Black Sisters' Street*   59
     Tomi Adeaga

5   Transnational African Women as Voices of Conscience: Aidoo's *Our Sister Killjoy*, Adichie's *Americanah*, and Atta's *A Bit of Difference*   73
     Nancy Henaku

6   Local and Global Perspectives on Nigerian Women's Activism in *News from Home* by Sefi Atta   89
     Rose A. Sackeyfio

7 Breaking Mythical Barriers through a Feminist Engagement
   with Magical Realism   103
   Elijah Adeoluwa Olusegun

Conclusion: Shifting the Boundaries of African Women's Writing   117
Rose A. Sackeyfio

Index   129

About the Contributors   137

Introduction
Rose A. Sackeyfio

TELLING THE AFRICAN STORY IN THE GLOBAL AGE

In the global age, female authors have moved beyond the margins of male-authored texts to command new spaces of prominence in the African literary canon. *African Women Writing Diaspora: Transnational Perspectives in the 21st Century* captures dynamic and progressive changes in the direction of the African novel such as the emergence of diaspora perspectives, and the success of leading third-generation women writers from Africa. A central theme in the literary imagination of contemporary female artists is thematic perspectives on the fluid and shifting constructions of African women's identity as female immigrants experience the intersection of race, class, and gender beyond the continent's borders.

The recent emphasis on contemporary themes of transnational identity is a compelling subject of debate as scholars, writers, and critics of African literature interrogate issues of authenticity, audience, language, and market-driven forces within Western spaces. Needless to say, the growing body of diaspora fiction crafted by women gives voice to their experiences of hybridity and their status as frequently marginalized others within transnational spaces. These works explore the puzzle of what it means to be African at home and abroad in the global world. Contemporary African women writers share the distinction of living in the West, which confers education and new and expanded opportunities along with paradoxical realities of *otherness*.

The origins of Anglophone African women's writing are credited to iconic literary pioneers such as Ama Ata Aidoo in 1965 with the publication of the play, *Dilemma of a Ghost*, followed by *Anowa* in 1970. Flora Nwapa is widely acknowledged as the mother of African women's literature through the groundbreaking publication of the novel *Efuru* in 1966. Mariama Ba, writing in French, crafted *So Long a Letter* (1979) rose to critical acclaim as a classic of Francophone African women's writing. These early works by African women are foundational within a literary tradition of feminist expression and postcolonial literature. The works foreground female voices that (re)imagined and corrected stereotypical images and monolithic representations of African women characters that appeared in male-authored texts such as Achebe's *Things Fall Apart* (1955), Wole Soyinka's *The Lion and the Jewel* (1959), and Cyprian Ekwensi's *Jagua Nana* (1961). The works of first-generationAfrican women illustrate their commitment to *write back*, to counter one-dimensional representations of females in literature. Madu Krishnan notes that:

> Nwapa's work may be read as a response to the masculinized discourses of her peers whose erasure of the feminine, in the name of nationalism, she sought redress through partial representation of tradition in which the feminine would be erased of its contradictions, instead celebrated as equally worthy of individuation and progression as the male. (2012: 9)

The image of women protagonists in fictional works was forever changed through the projection of strong, diverse, and complex characters that resist patriarchal oppression and barriers to their empowerment through their agency, strength, and resilience.

The London novels of Buchi Emecheta ushered the 1970s as a pivotal decade in the development and production of African women's fiction. Her works herald the introduction of *diaspora* as a new landscape of literary engagement to uncover the ways in which race and gender mediate women's everyday existence. The new and intriguing theme of African identity beyond the continent elaborates the literary history of African women's fiction that began with the aforementioned pioneering female authors, of whom Buchi Emecheta is the most prolific. As an important forerunner of Anglophone African women's writing, her legacy resonates in the literary expression of an entire generation of accomplished and successful women writers from Africa in the twenty-first century. Emecheta's importance as an iconic woman author began through publication of early works that chronicle the transformative nature of African diaspora life through a gendered lens. The autobiographical accounts of her life in London are vividly captured in her novels *In the Ditch* (1972), *Second Class Citizen* (1974), and *Kehinde* (1994). These texts are a window into the experience of female subjectivity through real-life accounts of patriarchal oppression in her marriage and socioeconomic status as a single parent of four children that unfold against the background of racialized identity in Britain, where she educated herself and produced an impressive literary corpus for over 20 years. Her final work, *The New Tribe* was published in 2000. In "Frames of Marginality: Emecheta's Legacy in the 21st Century," Sackeyfio succinctly confirms: Emecheta's importance in African, Nigerian, and women's writing inaugurates a dramatic shift in the direction of the African novel that continues to evolve in the twenty-first century (Sackeyfio, 2018: 25).

In 1977, Ama Ata Aidoo published *Our Sister Killjoy: Reflections of a Black-eyed Squint*. In the transnational space of Germany, the Ghanaian female at the center of the work enters the abrasive world of racial difference that fuels the author's critique of confused African identity and the impact of the colonial encounter. Similar to Emecheta, the brutal status of "other" is a salient theme that marks the tension between local and global realities that plague diaspora fictional narratives in African female-authored texts till the present.

The early years of the twenty-first century mark the celebration of women authors in the publication of *New Women's African Writing in African Literature*, Vol. 24 of *African Literature Today* in 2004. Ernest Emenyonu, in an editorial called "New Women's Writing: a Phenomenal Rise," applauds the dramatic increase in writing by African women. Most importantly, he notes that Buchi Emecheta published *The New Tribe* in 2000 that represents a shift in:

> vision and focus from the women on the African continent or African women transported to the Western world by sheer force of circumstance, to a new generation of Africans . . . who are citizens of the western world because they were born there to migrant parents. The focus now is on a new generation and a new social reality. Are these steadily growing new inhabitants Africans or are they "a new tribe of the western hemisphere?" This is the crux of the inquiry in Exile and Identity in Buchi Emecheta's *The New Tribe*. (2000: xiii)

In an interview with Yogita Goyal, author and critic Chris Abani boldly affirms that "it is beautiful that women dominate the new global placement of African literature; men dominated the first generation—that is a shift worth noting" (Abani, 2016: 229). Over the past two decades, African literature has moved dramatically beyond postcolonial themes of the emerging nation-state, cultural authenticity, and identity toward global issues of modern society in the flux. These ideas are expressed by imminent literary scholar and critic, the late Abiola Irele who notes that "a notable factor in the broadening of the horizons of the African novel entailed by these developments has been the remarkable entry of the women" (10).

Building upon diaspora perspectives, immigrant fiction produced by contemporary African women writers explore difficult and challenging questions that are expressed in an outpouring of vivid and insightful literature that spans two decades of the twenty-first century. The essays in this volume will address a range of themes in diaspora literature and some of the questions to consider are: How does the intersection of race, class, and gender influence the identity and status of African women living in the diaspora? How are feminist themes explored in African women's writing outside Africa? What is the relationship between African migrant women and African diaspora populations dispersed through enslavement? How do African women writers explore connections and perceptions of Africa as *homespace*? How do women writers project the image of African women in fictional works? How do African female authors interrogate the tensions between African cultural traditions and modernity in Western settings? How do African women writers (re)imagine African futures? How do writers depict African women and sexuality? And finally, how do women evolve agency to shape their destiny within marginalized spaces of Western environments? These questions and themes unify the volume as a meaningful contribution to literary criticism and engagement with "diaspora" as a dynamic and captivating trend in the evolution of the African novel.

Thus, African women's writing in the twenty-first century represents a connecting thread to the literary godmothers of the first generation. Diaspora fiction by women has exploded onto the literary stage and continues to expand into 2020 and beyond with highly visible, award-winning bestsellers consumed by largely Western audiences and celebrated internationally. In the wake of massive migration and flows from Africa that is stimulated by social, economic, and political transformation, significant immigrant populations reside outside her borders. Migration of Africans to Europe, America, and Asia has stimulated research and scholarship across a broad range of social science disciplines such as anthropology, sociology, geography, economics, history, and political science. Across the wide scope of disciplinary engagement, a rich body of research interrogates mobility, identity, and socioeconomic and legal status within foreign spaces. An exciting inter-disciplinary connection between the social sciences and the humanities is the importance of diaspora literary texts and the ways in which they mirror knowledge and research on human experience from the social science disciplines. Yoon Sun Lee corroborates the idea that "The key aspects of the diasporic imaginary highlighted in sociological and in theoretical accounts can also be found in the novels of diaspora" (2018: 196). Specifically, contemporary African women's diaspora fiction examines the complexities of women's identities outside Africa. The body of fictional works investigates the treatment of women, their status as diaspora subjects, racial identity, and hybridity to provide a holistic portrait that will re-(position) African women's agency in social interactions across national boundaries.

African Women Writing Diaspora: Transnational Perspectives in the 21st Century examines the fiction of many leading writers along with emerging authors of a first successful novel. With the exception of Ama Ata Aidoo, who has returned to Ghana, all of the writers whose works are analyzed reside in the west. The collection opens with Rose Sackeyfio's exploration of Yaa Gyasi's *Homegoing* (2016), which metaphorically captures the epic dimensions of the trauma of the Atlantic Slave Trade, plantation life in the American south, and return to Ghana generations later through the lens of gender. As a multigenerational work of historical fiction, this novel traces the lineage history of characters (male and female) that descended from two Ghanaian half-sisters, separated by the horror and trauma of Ghana's involvement in the slave trade. In 2016, Gyasi was awarded the National Book Foundations Prize, followed by the National Book Critic Circles John Leonard's Award for best first book. In 2017, Gyasi received the Hemingway Foundation/PEN Award. Sackeyfio highlights the ways in which the novel foregrounds the complexities of survival, memory, and return to Ghanaian cultural moorings as diaspora subjects negotiate survival, hybridity, and eventually experience a powerful reconnection to lost cultural heritage. As a first novel, Gyasi's work treats slavery, which is a subject that has only been written about in African women's fiction by none other than Ama Ata Aidoo in the play *Anowa* (1970). The work is a bold effort by Gyasi given the sensitive nature of slavery on both sides of the Atlantic. The novel may also be understood as an effort at reconciliation between Ghana and her diaspora and interestingly, themes of reconnection resonate in recent political and cultural events in Ghana when the president declared 2019 the "Year of Return" for the African diaspora. Sackeyfio's chapter highlights the importance of *memory* in reconnecting female diaspora subjects to their ancestral moorings in Ghana.

In a rare look at Francophone diaspora literature, Cheryl Toman's chapter "Malian Immigration in France: Perspectives from Women Writers of French Expression" examines the lives of Malian women immigrants that span the 1990s and the twenty-first century. The feminist perspectives of Calixthe Beyala, in *Loukoum: The Little Prince of Belleville* (1992) and Fatima Diallo's *Sous mon voile* "Under my Veil" (2015) unfold the challenges of immigrant life in France during two historical periods, the 1990s and 2015. Both works illustrate minimal changes in the perception and treatment of Malian immigrants during the 23 years between publication of the works. The realities of female subjectivity are conveyed through a realistic and vivid portrait of the challenges of the French-speaking Malian diaspora who face discrimination, unbelonging, and alienation in the effort to survive. The works capture the impact of discriminatory immigration policies on women's (and men's) legal status and family life and marriage in particular. Lydie Moudileno identifies Calixthe Beyela's work as "perhaps the most visible francophone African woman today, (who) also inaugurated the emergence in the 1980s of what some now call *Litteature migrante* ('migrant literature')."

These works represent the ways in which Francophone immigrant fiction unfold inter-connecting themes and sometimes they uncover the lives of the authors within diaspora spaces. With reference to Beyala's *The Little Prince of Belleville*, Toman asserts that:

> The family's ordeal and the stereotypes and prejudice that plague them seem typical in the Malian diaspora. Moreover, knowledge of the background of immigrant problems and legal barriers and constraints in France at the time makes this story even more disturbing and thus Beyala's novel achieves its purpose of exposing French society's numerous contradictions. (1995: 8)

Again, Toman skillfully juxtaposes spatiotemporal dimensions of ethnic hostility in France expressed in Diallo's autobiographical work as follows:

> Since the January 2015 attacks, people look at me more than ever. They are constantly staring me down. I can tell it's my veil that is the cause of this. I feel such strong tension in the street, in the subway. When I get on the train, I feel that no one trusts me as if I was going to commit a terrorist act, as if I were a criminal. (2015: 31)

Experiences of alienation and hostility capture the realism of Diallo's narrative to shed light on racial otherness as part of the everyday existence of Malian immigrant subjects.

Olusegun Elijah Adeoluwa's "Breaking Mythical Barriers through a Feminist Engagement with Magical Realism" takes readers into the world of speculative fiction and Afrofuturistic vision of Nigerian-American writer, Nnedi Okorafor. Through the lens of speculative fiction, African females construct new identities for themselves in *Who Fears Death* (2010) and *What Sunny Saw in the Flames* (2011). Zimbabwean science fiction writer and critic Ivor W. Hartmann affirms the importance of SciFi as a genre because it "enables African writers to envision a future from *our* African perspective. ... The value of this envisioning ... for our continent, cannot be overstated or negated. Thus, Science Fiction by African writers is of paramount importance to the development and future of our continent" (7). Speculative fiction offers an alternative space for extraordinary African superwomen to craft new identities in the landscapes of the future. Okorafor's imagination penetrates a genre dominated by male writers in the past as well as the present and breaks boundaries of gender identity within futuristic settings.

Adeoluwa's analysis illustrates the potential of speculative fiction to (re)imagine African female empowerment through what he calls "a blend of myths and histories of a non-Western culture and African culture in order to establish its settings as capable of supporting the fantasy narratives." In an interview called "To Be African Is to Merge Technology and Magic" Nnedi Okorafor states that: " she values the notion of Afrofuturism as a way of being for the indomitable female protagonists that so often populate the magical Nigerian landscapes of her stories" (2016: 207). The women characters at the center of each work embark on journeys, both symbolic and real, to uncover their "power" and to acquire knowledge about the power and structure of their society.

Okorafor's narrative style in both works is a skillfully crafted blend of African/Nigerian cultural traditions, myths, and practices along with the substance of Western-centered experience. Despite the other worldly settings that embody the "fantastical imaginary landscapes," Okorafor's artistry shines brightly through familiar vistas of African cultural moorings that are recast in the future. Adeoluwa highlights the feminist elements expressed by Okorafor's women characters in ways that foreground the centrality of African women as heroines who chart their own futures.

Okorafor is a successful writer of both young adult and adult novels, having published four novels, two children's books, and many short stories in recent years. As a prolific writer, her recognition and distinction are enormous and in 2008 she was awarded the Wole Soyinka Prize for *Zharah* the *Windseeker* (2005). Her novel *Who Fears Death* (2010) won the World Fantasy Award in 2011 and in 2007–2008, she received the MacMillan Writer's Prize for *Long JuJu Man* (2009). Finally, in 2016, she is the recipient of the Nebula Award for *Binti* (2015).

NoViolet Bulawayo is among the new and gifted African diaspora women writers whose debut novel *We Need New Names* (2016) is the focus of chapter 4 by Amanda Ladjii. Bulawayo migrated from Zimbabwe and *We Need New Names* is a tapestry of inter-locking themes of social, economic, and political chaos in Zimbabwe during the 1980s under the brutal oppression of the late Robert Mugabe. The first chapter of the novel titled "Hitting Budapest" has won the Caine Prize for African Writing in 2011. In 2014, Bulawayo won the Etisalat Prize for Literature and in the same year, the prestigious Hemingway Foundation/PEN Award for a first book. The novel earned the Los Angeles Times Book Prize in 2013.

"Waithood" and Girlhood in NoViolet Bulawayo's *We Need New Names* asserts that "postcolonial bildungsroman . . . exhibit characteristics of suspension and liminality similar to those identified by ethnographic studies of youth in the global South." Her interpretation of the novel suggests that temporality of "waiting" is central to the protagonists' diasporic experience. The novel unfolds through binary constructions that juxtapose the chaotic, dysfunctional, and bleak environment of Harare and the diaspora environment of Detroit (Destroyedmichygen), the past that informs the present, childhood, and adulthood modalities and the hybrid identity of the conflicted female protagonist that blur her future. As a coming of age tale, Lagjii positions the novel beyond classical bildungsroman to forge the genre within new contexts.

Tomi Adeaga's chapter 5 offers new insight into the dynamics of "Sexuality, Resilience and Mobility" in Amma Darko's *Beyond the Horizon* (1988) and Chika Unigwe's *On Black Sisters' Street* (2009). This chapter illuminates the puzzle of female sexuality as a form of modern-day slavery through human-trafficking as part of the global sex industry. Sexual objectification and commodification of the black female body has grown into a well-documented international enterprise of enormous proportions in the twenty-first century and thus represents the dark underbelly of "globalization." The novels are published decades apart but are linked by thematic exploration of African women's vulnerability to sexual exploitation in foreign spaces of Europe. In "Black Women's Bodies in a Global Economy: Sex, Lies and Slavery," Sackeyfio avers that "The structure of On Black Sisters' Street, goes beyond descriptions of the unwholesome nature of the sex trade to also reveal how patriarchal structures, poverty and desperation lead to bad choices among the restricted opportunities for women to survive by legitimate means" (202). Unigwe's novel is the result of research conducted in Belgium where she interviewed African sex workers as the basis of her novel *On Black Sisters' Street*. The novel is contrasted with Darko's tale of a naïve Ghanaian woman that is (mis)led into a life of prostitution by her deceitful husband. Similar to the women in *On Black Sisters' Street*, the diaspora space of Europe is risky and dangerous as women may be preyed upon by males and by economic forces over which they have little if any control.

Unigwe's works have established her among the leading contemporary African writers. Writing in Dutch and English, she is rated as one of Africa's top five writers, having won the 2012 Nigeria Prize for Literature for *On Black Sisters' Street* along with the Nigerian Liquefied Natural Gas (NLGP) Prize for literature in the same year.

In chapter 6, Rose Sackeyfio (re)positions "Local and Global Perspectives on Nigerian Women's Activism" in *News from Home* (2009) by Sefi Atta. The novella is part of her collection of short stories about Nigerian women. In the same way as the other fictional works examined in this collection, the central female character is torn between two worlds of "difference" that marks her initiation into "otherhood" in America. From the vantage point of the diaspora setting in New Jersey, she evolves a deeper sense of her identity, mirrored by the growing political consciousness of women in her community who awaken to activism in the Niger Delta. From New Jersey, she hears "news from home" about the environmental crisis caused by multinational oil drilling.

Through her transnational gaze, readers learn of pollution, disease, infertility, and economic stagnation that fuel local women's eco-feminist activism in defense of the environment. Sackeyfio traces the relationship between local and global realities and the evolution of women's agency in the effort to survive life's challenges at home and abroad. Sackeyfio unfolds the ways in which *News from Home* juxtaposes the awakened consciousness of women who take up the challenge to chart a new future in Africa and the diaspora. Sefi Atta is a critically acclaimed writer of four novels, *Everything Good Will Come* (2005), *Swallow* (2010), *A Bit of Difference* in (2013), and the publication of *The Bead Collector* in 2019. Her collection of short stories "*News from Home*" was published in 2009. She is also a successful playwright with several dramatic works to her credit. Atta is the recipient of the Wole Soyinka Award for Literature in 2006 for *Everything Good Will Come* the 2009 Noma Award for Publishing in Africa and the 2005 Pen International Award 1st Prize.

Nancy Henaku, in chapter 7, traces three fictional women characters in Atta's *A Bit of Difference* (2013), Aidoo's *Our Sister Killjoy* (1977), and Adichie's *Americanah* (2013) to foreground "Transnational African Women as Voices of Conscience." Her chapter looks at relationships between mobility, "gazing," and speaking. Henaku notes that the central women characters in the novels are able to become voices of conscience, writing and speaking back across borders because of their unique transnational positionality. Among the constellation of talented writers discussed in this chapter is Chimamanda Ngozi Adichie, widely acknowledged as the undisputed star of contemporary African literature. The late Chinua Achebe stated that: "We do not usually associate wisdom with beginners, but here is a new writer endowed with the gift of ancient storytellers. . . . She is fearless. . . . Adichie came almost fully made." Achebe's tribute to Adichie's talent symbolizes her importance as a writer whose influence spans the boundaries of the Igbo nation, Nigeria, Africa, and the West. She has authored three award-winning novels. *Purple Hibiscus* (2003) was one of the first of the three novels for which she was awarded the Commonwealth Writer's Prize for Best First Book.

Her second novel, *Half of a Yellow Sun* (2006) won the Orange Broadband Prize in 2007. The widely acclaimed *Americanah* (2013) received the National Book Critics Award in 2013 and in the same year she was named among the 100 most influential Africans. *The Thing Around Your Neck* (2009) is a collection of short fiction that focuses diaspora experiences of African women and in 2008 Adichie was the recipient of the MacArthur Genius Award. Her most recent work is a treatise on feminism in the twenty-first century, *We Should All be Feminists* published in 2014. Her awards and distinctions are too many to name and scholarly discourse on her fictional works have produced what can only be described as a formidable body of dissertations, literary studies, and inclusion in the literary canon of African, women's, and world literature internationally.

Unlike *Our Sister Killjoy,* the works by Atta and Adichie are recent publications, and themes of women's identity in foreign environments, the tensions between local and global forces, and return to Africa unite the works. Moreover, these elements link the feminist expression illustrated in Aidoo's *Our Sister Killjoy* as a novel representative of the first generation of African women writers outlined earlier. The inter-texual elements of the three novels highlight the (re)construction of African women's image to "unsilence" the subaltern. Henaku's chapter foregrounds what she calls "mobility and gaze" because "in all three narratives, mobility not only makes the protagonists aware of the power of the gaze, but also results in the development of oppositional consciousness and subaltern agency."

In reflection on the development of African diaspora literature by women who dominate the canon, leading African males are also producing excellent works that explore many of the same issues of race and class, hybridity, tradition and modernity, and relationships to Africa. Okey Ndibe's *Foreign Gods* (2016) narrates the failed American dream(s) of a male protagonist who drives a taxi for 13 years, although he earned top honors in his BA program at Amherst College. The novel unravels a dark ending through his foray into his village to steal and make quick profit from selling a piece of "art" back in United States. Teju Cole's *Open City* (2012) is a successful work that illustrates the intersecting realities of the male protagonist who journeys through a maze of diverse localities within his New York environment. Chris Abani's diaspora novella, *Becoming Abigail* (2006) unfolds a dark tale set in both Nigeria and London as young Abigail is betrayed into prostitution through trafficking. The bleakness of the novel lies in the young woman's search for identity beyond the sexual objectification that imprisons her existence as an undocumented migrant. Abani's *Virgin of the Flames* (2007) captures the odyssey of a confused Nigerian man searching for his sexual and racial identity in Los Angeles. His life is clouded by the loss of his father, distorted religious obsession and his uncertain future as a struggling artist. The *Beautiful Things that Heaven* Bears (2007) by Dinaw Mengestu chronicles the marginalized existence of an Ethiopian immigrant in Washington DC. The male character is torn between his Ethiopian roots and the depressing environment of his neighborhood in the throes of gentrification. The outpouring of African diaspora literature by female and male writers is a growing body of compelling works that push the boundaries of African literature in ways that arouse critical inquiry into the changing nature of the genre.

African Women Writing Diaspora: Transnational Perspectives in the 21st Century explores the fiction of many leading writers along with emerging authors of a first successful novel such as No Violet Bulawayo and Yaa Gyasi. The fictional works examined are unified through what Mukoma Wa Ngugi calls a *Rooted Transnationalism* (163) as a provocative turn in the evolution of the African novel in the age of globalization. In his book *The Rise of the African Novel* (2018) he argues that "We Need New Terms" for African literature to convey the transnational themes in the works that are informed by the diverse backgrounds of the writers. He posits that "in order to understand literature . . . it has to be through its transnational nature, which is also rooted in multiple cultures, nations and languages" (180). The characters in the "diaspora" works by African women authors are thus rooted in multiple localities. For example No Violet Bulawayo's *We Need New Names* spans Detroit and rural Zimbabwe. Likewise, the characters in Gyasi's *Homegoing* are connected to both Ghana and United States. The complexity and breadth of Adichie's *Americanah* unfold multiple sites of hybridity such as Nigeria, America, and Europe as characters navigate a landscape riddled with issues of race, class, and gender dynamics. Other sites of simultaneity in the works treated in the collection are Mali and France, America, Nigeria, and numerous African nations that are home to the trafficked sex workers in Unigwe's *On Black Sisters Street* in Belgium. These parameters hold true within Afrofuturistic landscapes that push the boundaries of reality, though (at least in the case of Nnedi Okorafor) is decidedly "rooted" in African sensibilities and cultural ethos.

Nonetheless, African literature as a category is forever transformed in the twenty-first century in ways that reflect the global age of massive mobility in the midst of social, economic, and political transformation. Helon Habila, in the African Literature Association Presidential Address in 2018 titled "The Future of African Literature," welcomes the "new wave of diasporic African literature as providing a new possibility, a way forward for African literature in general. A way out of the endless loop of nationalism and anti-colonialism, which keeps us trapped within the very structures of power we seek to oppose or correct" (159). Moreover, as a cultural product, literature illustrates that art not only reflects but creates and performs diasporic experiences" (Stierstorfer and Janet Wilson (xxii). The global landscape of transcultural mobility transmutes literary expression through the creative artistry of a new generation of women writers whose voices can never be silenced in telling the African story.

REFERENCES

Abani, Chris. 2004. *Graceland*. New York: Picador.
Abani, Chris. 2006. *Becoming Abigail: A Novella*. New York: Akashic.
Abani, Chris. 2007. *Virgin of the Flames*. New York: Penguin.
Achebe, Chinua. 1994. *Things Fall Apart 1959*. New York: Doubleday.
Adichie, Chimamanda Ngozi. 2004. *Purple Hibiscus*. Lagos: Farafina.

Adichie, Chimamanda Ngozi. 2007. *Half of a Yellow Sun.* Toronto: Alfred A. Knopf.
Adichie, Chimamanda Ngozi. 2009. *The Thing Around Your Neck.* Toronto: Alfred A. Knopf.
Adichie, Chimamanda Ngozi. 2013. *Americana.* Toronto: Alfred A. Knopf.
Aidoo, Ama Ata. 1965. *Dilemma of a Ghost and Anowa.* England: Longman.
Aidoo, Ama Ata. 1977. *Our Sister Killjoy: Or Reflections of a Black-Eyed Squint.* Lagos/New York: Nok Press.
Aidoo, Ama Ata. 2012. *Diplomatic Pounds & Other Stories.* UK: Ayebia Clarke.
Atta, Sefi. 2010. *News from Home.* North Hampton: Interlink Books.
Atta, Sefi. 2013. *A Bit of Difference.* Northampton: Interlink Books.
Atta, Sefi. 2019. *The Bead Collector.* UK: The New Internationalist.
Beyala, Calixthe. 1995. "Lettre d'une Africaine à ses sœurs occidentales." Paris: Spengler, *Loukoum: The "Little Prince" of Belleville,* translated by Marjolijn de Jager. Portsmouth: Heinemann.
Bulawayo, NoViolet. 2013. *We Need New Names.* New York: Regan Arthur Books.
Cole, Teju. 2011. *Open City.* New York: Random House.
Diallo, Fatimata. 2015. *Sous mon voile.* Paris: Seuil.
Ekwensi, Cyprian. 1961. *Jagua Nana.* London: Heinemann.
Emecheta, Buchi. 1972. *In the Ditch.* London: Barrie and Jenkins.
Emecheta, Buchi. 1974. *Second Class Citizen.* New York: George Braziller.
Emecheta, Buchi. 1994. *Kehinde.* London: Heinemann.
Emecheta, Buchi. 2000. *The New Tribe.* Heinemann: London.
Emenyonu, Ernest. 2004. "New Women's Writing: A Phenomenal Rise." Editorial Article. *New Women's Writing in African Literature,* Vol. 24, edited by Ernest Emenyonu (xi). Oxford: James Curry.
Goyal, Yogita. 2014. "A Deep Humanness, a Deep Grace: Interview with Chris Abani." *Research in African Literatures,* Vol. 45, No. 3, Africa and the Black Atlantic (Fall) 227–240.
Gyasi, Yaa. 2016. *Homegoing.* New York: Vintage Books.
Habila, Helon. 2018. "The Future of African Literature." ALA Presidential Address. *Journal of the African Literature Association,* Vol. 13, No. 1, 153–162.
Hartmann, Ivor W. 2012. *AfroSF: Science Fiction by African Writers,* edited by Ivor W. Hartman. A Storytime Publication.
Irele, Abiola. 2009. "Introduction: Perspectives on the African Novel." *The Cambridge Companion to the African Novel,* edited by Abiola Irele. 1–29. UK: Cambridge University Press.
Krishnan, Madhu. 2012. "Mami Wata and the Occluded Feminine in Anglophone Nigerian-Igbo Literature." *Research in African Literatures,* Vol. 43, No. 1, 1–18.
Lee, Yun Sun. 2018. "The Postcolonial Novel and Diaspora." *The Routledge Diaspora Studies Reader,* edited by Klaus Stierstorfer and Janet Wilson. 96–200. London: Routledge.
Mengetsu, Dinaw. 2007. *The Beautiful Things That Heaven Bears.* New York: Riverhead.

Moudileno, Lydie. 2009. "The Francophone Novel in Sub-Saharan Africa." *The Cambridge Companion to the African Novel*, edited by Abiola Irele. 125–139. UK: Cambridge University Press.
Ndibe, Okey. 2014. *Foreign Gods Inc.* New York: Soho Press.
Nwapa, Flora. 1966. *Efuru*. London: Heinemann.
Okorafor, Nnedi. 2010. *Who Fears Death*. New York: Daw Books.
Okorafor, Nnedi. 2011. *What Sunny Saw in the Flames*. Abuja: Cassava Republics.
Okorafor, Nnedi. 2016. "To Be African Is to Merge Technology and Magic." An Interview with Nnedi Okorafor. *Afrofuturism 2.0: The Rise of Astro-Blackness*, edited by Anderson Reynold and Charles E. Jones, Vol. 2. 201–213. Lanham: Lexington Books.
Sackeyfio, Rose. 2014. "Black Women's Bodies in a Global Economy: Sex, Lies and Slavery." *At the Crossroads: Readings of the Postcolonial and the Global in African Literature and Visual Art*, edited by Ghirmai Negash, Andrea Frohne, and Samuel Zadi. 202–219. Trenton: Africa World Press.
Sackeyfio, Rose. 2018. "Frames of Marginality: Emecheta's Legacy in the 21st Century." *Praxis: Journal of Gender and Cultural Critique*, Vol. 26, No. ½, Spring/Fall 21–34.
Soyinka, Wole. 1962. *The Lion and the Jewel*. London: Oxford University Press.
Wa Ngugi, Mukoma. 2018. *The Rise of the African Novel: Politics of Language, Identity, and Ownership*. 163–118. Ann Arbor: University of Michigan Press.

Chapter 1

Memory, Identity, and Return in Yaa Gyasi's *Homegoing*

Rose A. Sackeyfio

Yaa Gyasi's *Homegoing* (2016) is an epic work of historical fiction that narrates the experiences of Ghanaian and diaspora people whose lives are shaped by the legacy of enslavement, displacement, and fractured cultural heritage. As an emerging Ghanaian writer, Gyasi weaves a tapestry of gendered realities that portray the complexities of female subjectivity in pre-colonial Ghana and the American South as a salient theme. This chapter traces the transformative experiences of memory, resilience, and identity as Ghanaian women characters and their descendants respond to their oppression and exploitation and the intersection of race, class, and gender. This chapter examines contemporary questions about diasporic communities, cultural continuity, and survival. An important feature of Gyasi's account is the skillfully crafted portrayal of Ghanaian women's agency and the ability to negotiate the barriers to equality during the brutal assault on their humanity in the spatiotemporal nexus of connecting the past and the present.

Homegoing re-creates a holistic portrait of Ghanaian women characters to construct a counter-narrative to images of voiceless and dis-empowered women. The novel disrupts conventional monolithic images of Ghanaian/African women that are cast simply as "the slaves" in ways that foreground cultural identity, strength, and memory of the past. The act of (re)membering is expressed in the survival of familial bonds, symbolism, and racial identity in America that motivate sentiments of longing and return to Ghanaian cultural moorings. Yaa Gyasi displays compelling insight into the dynamics of Ghanaian and diaspora connections in ways that interrogate the reconciliation of centuries-old rupture of Africa and her diaspora in the twenty-first century. The spatiotemporal dimensions of the novel are structured in two parts that describe slave trading in Ghana and the diaspora setting in Alabama, Baltimore, and New York. The broad scope of the work is reminiscent of

Olaudah Equiano's recollections of Igbo culture and way of life before his capture at age 10. Each chapter unfurls the life of one of the descendants of the two sisters. The events are cyclical, as the novel ends in Ghana, where it began, at the Cape Coast castle on the shores of the Atlantic ocean.

MEMORY AS HISTORY

As an overarching theme in the novel, *memory,* both literal and figurative, pervades the experiences of the female characters that are linked by Asante culture, as women recall Ghana as homeland. *Homegoing* is framed by the infamous Elmina Castle as a site of remembrance and reconnection of African diaspora people to Ghanaian cultural origins. The novel situates the lineage history of the sisters at Elmina Castle as an anchor to an important historical site and cultural link to the descendants of dispersed peoples through the Atlantic slave trade. Since her independence from Britain in 1957, Ghana has been attracting people of color because of her commitment to inviting African Americans and other diaspora peoples to re-connect to the motherland as a place of homage. The importance of *Homegoing* as a way to engage discourse between Ghana and the African diaspora cannot be overstated. As a work of historical fiction that was published in 2016, the novel presages the declaration of 2019 as the *Year of Return* by Ghana's president, Nana Afuko-Addo. Gyasi's fiction offers a view into historical events that bridge multiple divides caused by the Atlantic slave trade as a route to remembrance of the African past.

Through women's narrative voices, Gyasi recreates what Lean'tin Bracks calls "historic memory" from the perspective of powerless females who tell their stories of pain and suffering. Spanning 300 years, the work traces the lineage of two half-sisters, Effia and Esi, that foreground the gendered perceptions of female experiences of enslavement, brutality, and sexual exploitation during the Atlantic Slave trade. Against her will, Effia is married to a British Governor as a wench/wife in a union arranged primarily by her stepmother. She and other "wives" of the British soldiers live in the castle, initially unaware of the human cargo housed below in the dungeons. Temporality marks the structure of the novel that stretches across several generations and the early recollections of traumatic separation of mothers and daughters are couched in a special black stone passed down to women descended from both half-sisters. As a reoccurring motif, the stone is symbolic of remembrance, ancestral linkage, and maternal bonds that translate ethnic identity across the ages.

Among the Asante community, Effia is married and upon leaving her people, she is given a Black stone pendant that represents "a piece of her mother" (Gyasi, 2016: 16). Generations later, and still in Ghana, her descendant, Abena, frustrated and denied acceptance and status as a married woman, leaves her father's village seeking liberation and a new identity. She seeks freedom, not from slavery but from marginalization in her community. Before she leaves, her father retrieves the buried black stone necklace and tells her, " This belonged to your great-grandmother Effia. It was given to her by her own mother" (Gyasi, 2016: 152). To Abena, this is the first time she had heard the name of one of her ancestors and, in "savoring the taste of the name on her tongue . . . she wanted to say it again and again. . . . She touched the stone to her neck and said thank you to her ancestors" (Gyasi, 2016: 152–153). These events evoke the central motif in the novel through the act of (re)membering the past as a bridge to the future.

The lives of the sisters unfold different destinies that are unknown to either of the women who become separated by fate. An ironic twist unfolds the story of Esi (half-sister to Effia) when her village is raided, and her mother, Maame, gives her a black stone. She is traumatized by her terrifying capture at age 15, enslavement, rape, and brutal treatment in the dungeons of Elmina castle. Esi, along with others, is kidnapped by Fante soldiers and eventually sold into slavery. Her suffering and resilience are vividly etched against the possession of the black stone as the only material symbol of her maternal lineage, her people, and her country. Held captive in the dungeons, it is the stone that she struggles to retain against impossible odds. When Esi is knocked to the ground by British soldiers for spitting at one of the Fante slave traders, she swallows the stone and later retrieves it from the ankle-deep waste on the floor of the dungeon after passing it out of her body.

Unfortunately, she and the other female captives are herded onto a slave ship bound for America and she departs without the stone. Symbolic of memory, lineage, survival, and regeneration of Ghanaian identity, the stone reappears to her descendant in the final chapter of the novel, thus, completing a cycle of *homegoing* to Cape Coast as the site of historical cleavage. Significantly, not only is the stone black, it "glimmers with gold" (Gyasi, 2016: 42). The rich imagery invokes the wealth of the Ashanti Empire, renown since the eleventh century, inspiring the British to rename the nation the "Gold Coast" as the setting of colonial domination and exploitation.

Gyasi structures the lineage histories of the sisters to suggest the possibility of recovery and reconnection to Africa for diaspora subjects. Despite historical amnesia and severed consciousness of ancestral origins, unexplained longing for knowledge of the past may surface and become the motivation to seek one's origins. Throughout the novel, Esi's descendants experience the trauma of ruptured history represented by the loss of the stone. Ironically, three generations later, her great, great-grandson is (re)connected with his blood kin on the shores of the Atlantic Ocean in Cape Coast Ghana where the stone is described as having "glints of gold ... shining in the sun" (Gyasi, 2016: 300) when it is given to Marcus, Esi's descendant.

Further, *memory* of African origins resonates in retention of indigenous Ghanaian language among females struggling to survive the brutality of plantation life in America. The story of Esi evokes Asante identity in speaking the forbidden Twi to her daughter Ness:
Esi:

> had spoken to her in Twi until their master caught her. He'd given Esi five lashes, for every Twi word Ness spoke, and when Ness, seeing her battered mother, had become too scared to speak, he gave Esi five lashes for each minute of Ness's silence. Before the lashes, her mother had called her Maame, after her own mother, but the master had whipped Esi for that too. (Gyasi, 2016: 71)

Memory haunts the experiences of the female characters that are linked through kinship to future generations in the diaspora. Ness's memories bind her to pain and loss, and as Esi's daughter, her life as an enslaved woman is the most brutal of all the horrors inflicted on the characters in the work. Gyasi presents a vivid and gripping account of violence, sacrifice, and struggle to survive under life-threatening conditions on the slave plantation. Esi is sold in 1796, ripped from the arms of her mother. Her remembrance of Ghana is recollected in the bedtime stories told to her as a child by her mother about:

> 'the Big Boat.' Ness would fall asleep to the images of men being thrown into the Atlantic Ocean like anchors attached to nothing: no land, no people, no worth. In the Big Boat, Esi said, they were stacked ten high, and when a man died on top of you, his weight would press the pile down like cooks pressing garlic. (Gyasi, 2016: 70)

Though fragmented, these remembrances crystallize when Ness anticipates another public spectacle of punishment years later on another plantation.

The gruesome scars on Ness's back mark the violence against the black female body as a text of pain. Of the two plantations she has lived on in Alabama; the first is described as "Hell" and the slave master is the "Devil." When she is paired with a male slave called Sam, she makes a sacrifice that almost costs her life. Sam is a new arrival from the continent, does not speak English, and is openly rebellious. In a fit of rage, he destroys the slave quarters and in an act of personal sacrifice, Ness accepts the blame and is almost beaten to death by the slave master.

> Her scarred skin was like another body in and of itself, shaped like a man hugging her from behind with his arms hanging around her neck. They went up

from her breasts, rounded the hills of her shoulders, and travelled the full, proud length of her back.... Ness's skin was no longer skin really, more like the ghost of her past made seeable, physical. (Gyasi, 2016: 74)

The slave narratives mirror the lived experiences as well as eye-witness accounts of bestiality against enslaved Black women meted out by sadistic slave masters as punishment that represents what Jennifer Putzi calls the legacy of the marked black body (Gyasi 2). In her article "'Raising the Stigma': Black Womanhood and the Marked Black Body in Pauline Hopkins's" *Contending Forces*, she notes the degrading nature of the scars received from whipping as a form of "stigma." During slavery, there was no division of labor among female and male slaves, and the physical abuse suffered by women was no less severe than beatings and torture of enslaved males. The black female body was vulnerable, with no form of protection from her fellow enslaved males, thus subject to public exposure, humiliation, violence, and sexual abuse.

Mary Prince's *The Life of a West Indian Slave* (1831) reveals unbridled cruelty through graphic descriptions, narrated by Prince as the first slave narrative published in Great Britain. Her recollections of scarring from the whippings and beatings illustrate the depraved mentality of the slave master, Mr. Woods and his wife. Mary was owned by four masters and observed that she is essentially "going from one butcher to another" (10). The story of Hetty, a fellow slave being repeatedly stripped naked and hung by her hands while pregnant, takes on monstrous dimensions of human debasement and iniquity. The woman delivers a stillborn child and later dies (Prince, 1831: 262–263).

Writing in 1845, Frederick Douglass shares the horrors of violence against enslaved women. As a boy, Douglass recalls:

I have often been awakened at dawn of day by the most heart-rending shrieks of an aunt of mine, whom (Master) used to tie up to a joist, and whip upon her naked back till she was literally covered with blood.... The louder she screamed the harder he whipped; and where the blood ran fastest, there he longest. (Douglass, 1845: 343–344)

Douglass reflects that witnessing his aunt being whipped with such incomprehensible cruelty "was the blood-stained gate, the entrance to the hell of slavery, through which I was about to pass" (Douglass, 1845: 539).

Gyasi portrays characters that have Asante names as a marker of ethnic origins during the crippling trauma of enslavement. Ness names her son Kojo (born on Monday). The survival of indigenous Ghanaian names among enslaved communities as portrayed in the work appears contrary to the well-documented historical evidence of new names being given during a "seasoning process" in the Caribbean before re-sale of African captives in North America. This liminal period is part of the triangular trade route as a prelude to plantation life in the American south. In *African American Odyssey* (2009), Darlene Hines notes that:

> seasoning was a disciplinary process intended to modify the behavior and attitude of slaves and make them effective laborers. As part of this process, the slaves' new masters gave them new names: Christian names, generic African names, or names from classical Greece and Rome ... the seasoning process also involved slaves learning European languages. (2009: 45)

Further, Alex Haley in his semi-autobiography, *Roots: The Saga of an American Family* (1976), claimed remembrance of an African name in his family (Kunta Kinte) that allowed him to trace his lineage to the West African nation of Gambia. However, the authenticity of his account is disputed by genealogists and historians. Moreover, *The Interesting Life of Olaudah Equiano* (1789) recalls the life of the only known survivor of the Middle Passage as a well-documented account of retention of African ethnic origins. Olaudah is Igbo and recalls his capture at age 10 in Nigeria and being sold into slavery. As an adult, he gains his freedom in Great Britain and writes a powerful and detailed account of Igbo life before his enslavement. Moreover, with regard to retention of ancestral languages in the Americas, Darlene Hines (et al.) says of African languages that they:

> contributed to the pidgins and creolized languages that became Black English by the nineteenth century.... The Gullah and Geechee dialects of the sea islands of South Carolina and Georgia, which combine African words and some African grammatical elements ... are still spoken today. (68)

Further, Emory S. Campbell notes the groundbreaking work of Lorenzo Dow Turner in 1949 as a masterpiece of linguistic research that substantiates the origins of Gullah-Geechee dialect in Georgia as derived from the Mende language in Sierra Leone. Turner listed many names and commonly used words of African origin (2006: 78). Likewise, Jermaine Archer corroborates the retention of cultural memories in slave narratives in the antebellum south that include "references to the religious and spiritual world from which they came ... that demonstrate the persistence of memory within the slave quarters" (2006: 85).

Nevertheless, despite the survival of diverse cultural retentions such as those found in African American musical expression, foods, spiritual traditions, and family patterns, African languages did not survive in ways that connect diaspora people to specific family lineage in their ethnic communities of origin.

RESISTANCE AND IDENTITY

Enslaved women's agency to gain their freedom is illustrated when Ness takes the initiative to flee the plantation with the assistance of Aku, who "knew the way back out" of slavery as she had "taken children north before" (Gyasi, 2016: 85).

The women are connected through language that becomes a route to survival and Asante women's identity. Aku is a woman whose heroism animates the memory of Harriet Tubman through rescue of enslaved Africans through the Underground Railroad in America. In church, Ness began singing a Twi tune sang by her mother and Aku recognizes the song. She tells Ness "So you are an Asante and you don't even know" (Gyasi, 2016: 84).

This experience educes the work of Joseph Opala in the documentary film *The Language You Cry In* (1989) that traces the remembrance of a Mende song passed down among women in the Moran family for generations. Opala based his work on Lorenzo Dow Turner, recorded it, and replayed it in Sierra Leone where it was recognized by the local women as a Mende song for funeral rituals (Campbell, 2011: 81).

These examples are a reminder of the power of *memory* to bridge the past and the present, sometimes through recollections that appear insignificant.

The discovery of another Asante woman on the plantation is pivotal to Ness's consciousness, identity, and remembrance of her people before capture. Aku had been kept in the castle just like Ness's mother, before being shipped to the Caribbean and then to America (Gyasi, 2016: 85). Aku's role is emblematic of Black women's resistance to oppression because she "had taken Akan people north to freedom many times, so many times that she had earned the Twi nickname *Nyame Nsa*, 'hand of God,' of help" (Gyasi 85). Retention of linguistic origins invigorate strategies of resistance on multiple levels as enslaved women recover remnants of Ghanaian matrilineal identity in the work.

Tragically, the escape plan is foiled as Ness and her husband Sam are recaptured while Aku and baby Kojo escape to Baltimore. Thus, Ma Aku emerges as a towering figure whose courage and resilience span the slave community in Alabama to greater freedom in Maryland. Ma Aku was like a mother to Kojo and fictive kin relationships were common during enslavement. Years later as an adult, Kojo recollects that Ma Aku:

> would never leave Baltimore. Unless she could go back to the Gold Coast. . . . Once the woman had decided to get free, she had also decided to stay free. When he was a child, Jo would often marvel at the knife Ma Aku always kept tucked inside of her wrapper since her days as an Asante slave, then an American slave, then finally free, The older Jo got, the more he understood

that sometimes staying free required unimaginable sacrifice. (Gyasi, 2016: 120)

When Kojo's wife disappears in Baltimore, Ma Aku speaks to him in *Twi*:

You will make it through this, . . . Nyame (the Akan name for God) did not make weak Asantes, and that is what you are, no matter what man here, white or black, wishes to erase that part of you. Your mother came from strong, powerful people. People who do not break. (Gyasi, 2016: 130)

As a source of moral and spiritual support, Ma Aku becomes an anchor of strength and comfort to Kojo. When he would worry that his family line had been cut off because he lost his parents in the south, "she would tell him stories about nations. The Fantes of the Coast, the Asante's of the Inland, the Akan people of Ghana" (Gyasi, 2016: 130). Essentially, this represents individual as well as collective memories and Kojo recalls that Ma Aku was still dreaming of the country she had been ripped from years and years before. She could often be found looking out at the water.

Despite the fragmented nature of stories, accounts of past experiences and genealogy, these types of recollections were a source of resistance to oppression and an aid to survival among enslaved people. Lean'tin Bracks affirms "The meaning of surviving and confronting an existence of subjugation . . . is found in the historical memories preserved in legacies, traditions, and rituals kept alive in the black community" (1998: 9).

Further, Bracks asserts that "ancestral memory . . . has served as both protection from and guidance through the outside world and preserver of experiences within the community for people with African roots" (1998: 20).

Ma Aku's role as the moral and spiritual center of her family and community is mirrored in the literature of leading African American female authors who celebrate the significance of the grandmother figure. Indeed, African American families and communities simulated many features of African life such as extended families, mutual assistance, and moral support.

African and African diaspora family patterns replicate matriarchal roles that foreground guidance, wisdom, and strength in the interest of loved ones. In the past as well as the present, grandmothers appear as a pivotal figure throughout all literary genres that span the historical landscape of enslavement, emancipation, and the challenge of survival of the black family into the twenty-first century. She appears in poetry, plays, short stories, autobiographies, and novels. In both life and literature, grandmothers represent stability, unity, continuity, and a repository of spiritual strength. The resourceful qualities of African American grandmothers evolve a wellspring of enduring strength that enables loved ones to survive adversity and oppression. The tenacity of the grandmother figure emerges through richly textured narratives in African American literary classics such as in Harriet Jacob's *Incidents in the Life of a Slave Girl* (1861). Jacobs brings to life the enduring qualities of her grandmother whom she:

> 'feared as well as loved' because of her deep religious commitment. . . . Moreover, she was a woman of high spirit. She was usually very quiet in her demeanor; but if her indignation was once aroused, it was not easily quelled. I had been told that she once chased a white gentleman with a loaded pistol, because he insulted one of her daughters. I dreaded the consequences of a violent outbreak. (Jacobs, 1861: 6)

Maya Angelou's autobiography profiles Annie Henderson as her grandmother in *I Know Why the Caged Bird Sings* (1969). Maya and her brother are sent to live with her and despite dangerous racial tension in Stamps Arkansas. Annie Henderson emerges with dignity and courage as a successful businesswoman during a period of intense economic hardship and oppression. Mama Lena Younger in Lorraine Hansberry's *A Raisin in the Sun* (1959) is a devoted matriarch, who guides her family through strong values to secure their future. Gloria Naylor's grandmother in *Mama Day* (1988) is a powerful healer and protector of her granddaughter Cocoa. She is highly respected in her community and will stop at nothing to care for her loved ones. Miranda Day's influence and authority may be traced to West African women's spiritual traditions and role in society (Levine, 2003: 27). The intertextual elements of the works rebound in ways that historicize women's identity through generations of black women's fiction as well as autobiography that spans the African diaspora experience. Gyasi adroitly traces the salient features of women's identities that connect characters in *Homegoing* like Ma Aku and Akua, to strong females portrayed in the works of Jacobs, Angelou, Hansberry, and Naylor. In all the works, the grandmothers navigate survival strategies, endurance, and resistance in the midst of conflict, adversity, and barriers to racial equality. Indeed, the grandmother role is one of the strongest and most significant African cultural retentions among African descended peoples scattered throughout the diverse settings of the diaspora that is still common among people of color all over the world.

In reconstructing Ghanaian historiography, Gyasi pays tribute to the memory of the Asante Warrior Queen Mother, Yaa Asantewa, who is referenced in the text although she is not a character in the work. Her leadership in the "War for the Golden Stool" (March 28, 1900) also known as the "War of Yaa Asantewaa Independence" against the British is well known, widely documented, and still memorialized as part of Ghana's rich cultural heritage. Gyasi commemorates the impact of Yaa Asantewa as a freedom fighter who inspires resistance to the invasion of the British: Nana Serwa is described as keeping a knife in her bed and:

> After the Queen Mother's call to arms reached Edweso, she had pulled that machete out from the bed and taken it with her into the compound. And all the men who had not already gone to fight for the Asante took one look at the old woman holding the large weapon and left. And so began the war. (Gyasi, 2016: 183)

The significance of her role is especially relevant because the Asante are a matrilineal society, distinguished by the survival of the Queen Mother system beyond the colonial assault that ended in 1957 when Ghana became independent of the United Kingdom. The Queen Mother system exists today in the twenty-first century as an expression of African matriarchy and indigenous roles of women that confer power and authority.

RECLAIMING THE PAST

Three generations later, Marjorie finds her way home from Alabama to Cape Coast as a descendant of her aged grandmother Akua in Ghana. The old woman is a spiritually charged figure, carrying stories of the past, engraved in the scars on her body and etched in the echoes of the past suffering of her family and her community. When Marjorie "was born, thirteen years ago, . . . her parents had mailed her umbilical cord to Old Lady so that the woman could put it into the ocean" (Gyasi, 2016: 267). The Old Lady had requested that if her son and daughter-in-law "ever had a child they would send something of that child back to Ghana" (Gyasi, 2016: 267) from America. The ritual of burying the umbilical cord and placenta is practiced throughout Africa and in many parts of the world. It is intended not only to restore fertility and to aid in healing the womb but also to bind the child's spirit to the earth and to ensure that the child returns home. The old woman puts the umbilical cord into the water so that if Marjorie's spirit ever wandered, she would know where home was.

Homegoing resonates the idea of "return," embodied in Marjorie who comes of age in America. Gyasi skillfully weaves the symbolic elements of Marjorie's and her grandmother's relationship when she visits Ghana every summer, especially when she is urged to speak Twi. They share a "summer ritual" of going to the ocean, an experience that Marjorie cherishes deeply. Akua asks her if she is wearing the black stone that bears the ancestral history of her family. Her grandmother reminds her that the stone had belonged to "Old Lady, and to Abena before her, and to James, and Quey, and Effia the

Beauty before that. . . . She is told never to take it off and significantly it is described as 'reflecting the ocean water before them, gold waves shimmering in the black stone'" (Gyasi, 2016: 267).

The compelling experiences that re-connect Marjorie to Asante identity in Ghana are sharply juxtaposed with her alienation back in Alabama. Marjorie comes of age to racial dynamics as she is torn between her Ghanaian identity at home and the abrasive realities of *blackness* in America. She knows she is unlike the African Americans in school and in her neighborhood, and she is called "white" because of her speech and behaviors. Cultural and racial difference is driven home to Marjorie through difficult experiences of *otherness*, especially painful in a failed inter-racial relationship. When her teacher asks her to share her feelings about being an African American, Marjorie is puzzled and recalls *Akata as* the Ghanaian word for "African American" used at home.

Marjorie's feelings of "unbelonging" convey the dichotomy between continental Africans and the diaspora who may clash within the racially charged environment in America as the legacy of enslavement. Marjorie's teacher tells her "here in this country, it doesn't matter where you came from first to the white people running things. You're here now. And here black is black is black" (Gyasi, 2016: 273). Recent decades have witnessed a massive influx of African immigrants in America, causing the stark realization of *blackness* that arise from America's dark history of racial oppression and, essentially, identity based on skin color. African immigrants are thrown into this mix, forcing them to reinvent their status and identity as black Africans. Halters and Showers-Johnson in *African and American: West Africans in Post-Civil Rights America* (2014) observe: the process "ethnicization in recent decades, . . . whereby the factors of both nationality *and* race figure significantly when members of the new West African diaspora proceed to negotiate and re-create their status in their adopted homeland" (2014: 256).

Marjorie's discomfort with being called African American resonates with Nigerian writer Chimamanda Ngozi Adiche's often quoted articulation of identity politics expressed in "Learning to be Black." Moreover, in her bestseller *Americanah* (2013), the Nigerian protagonist Ifemelu addresses her fellow African immigrants in her blog:

> Dear Non-American Black, when you make the choice to come to America, you become black. Stop arguing. Stop saying I'm Jamaican or I'm Ghanaian. America doesn't care. So what if you weren't 'black' in your country? You're in America now. We all have our initiation into the society of former Negroes. (Adichie, 2013: 222)

Adichie highlights the root cause of the dichotomy among African-born immigrants and the African diaspora that takes on a life of its own in the form of denial, rejection, ignorance, and conflict. Diverse historical experiences of dispersal of Africans in foreign lands have ruptured African diaspora ethnic identity, forging, a vast gulf across time and space in the black Atlantic. Marjorie's relationship with her grandmother in Ghana is thus a bridge to self- acceptance, recognition, and reconnection to the past. The transformative energies of (re)membering, inspires Marjorie's poem:

Split the Castle open
Find me, find you.
We, two, felt sand. (Gyasi, 2016: 282)

The theme of duality expressed in the poem suggests the two sisters, the past and the present, Ghana and the diaspora as Marjorie comes to terms with her identity.

The poem conveys the separation of the two sisters while the slave castle evokes the spatiotemporal framing of their diverging paths in life. The idea that they are so near, yet unknown to each other in the castle, resonates the trauma of erasure and *forgetting* through the formation of the African diaspora.

Eventually, Marjorie's grandmother dies and she and her family travel to Ghana for the funeral where, overcome by grief, Marjorie calls the name of her maternal ancestor, *Maame*.

Gyasi interrogates historical continuity of Ghana and the diaspora to invoke healing of the fissures created by the slave trade. The novel ends with reconnection of the descendants of Esi and Effia whose destinies originated in Cape Coast. Marcus is a young man searching for his fractured past, represented in the absence of the black stone that was lost on the floor of the dungeon of Cape Coast castle by his ancestor. In a twist of fate, Marcus meets Marjorie through fortuitous circumstances. He carries his own *memories* that surface when he is with his family and his grandmother, Ma Willie who suggests that he had the "gift of visions." He would imagine a hut in Africa, a patriarch holding a machete; sometimes outside in a forest of palm trees, a crowd watching a young woman carrying a bucket on her head (Gyasi, 2016: 290).

Marcus searches for his past through research and writing and he knew instinctively that his life represented the accumulated experiences of his ancestral lineage and the times during which they lived, spanning generations since slavery.

The novel comes full circle when Marjorie and Marcus return to Ghana as the descendants of the two sisters. They visit Cape Coast castle and enter the part of the dungeons where female captives were held centuries ago before they are hauled onto the slave ships. Final scenes are in the castle, and in the waters of the Atlantic ocean. The cleansing and healing powers of the water wash away the unforgiving past of slavery, pain and fractured lineage ties. As a curative gesture to suture the bonds of kinship, Marjorie gives the black stone necklace to Marcus. In *Migrations of Identity,* Carol Boyce Davies says of diaspora people:

> We are products of separations and dis-locations and dis-memberings, people of African descent in the Americas historically have sought reconnection. . . . This need to re- connect and re-member, as Morrison would term it has been a central impulse in the structuring of Black thought. (1994: 17)

In conclusion, *Homegoing* is a vivid rendering of ancestral lineage, historiography, continuity, the holocaust and trauma of enslavement, and African women's identities. The novel is a masterful work that conveys the transformative experiences of displacement, and the complexities of survival within and outside the boundaries of community in Ghana and America. There are many acts of remembrance in the work that compel diaspora subjects to find their way homeward and to reconcile the legacy of the past. The work gives voice to women, to counter images of voiceless figures held captive by their oppression before, during, and after enslavement. *Homegoing* commemorates the strength and resilience of women on both sides of the Atlantic, to persevere, and to protect their families and communities through diverse forms of resistance and the sheer will to survive. The complexity of *Homegoing* lies in the depth of the author's insight into women's and men's capacity to survive horrific experiences of trauma, loss and dehumanization meted out in Ghana and the Americas.

The novels' theme of return to ancestral origins gestures to the possibility of reconciliation among diaspora communities and continental Africans. Gyasi has created powerful imagery of the black stone that "glimmers with gold" as a vivid symbol of the rich cultural heritage of Ghanaian people that is rooted in the consciousness of descendants for generations. Gyasi illustrates the human potential to overcome the legacy of slavery and to move beyond eroded cultural identity in the distant past. The characters in the novel come alive through their humanity that shines through their strength and the ties that bind them to their loved ones. The search for identity brings the novel full circle to Ghanaian cultural moorings that connect the past, present, and future.

REFERENCES

Adichie, Chimamanda Ngozi. 2013. *Americanah*. Toronto: Alfred A. Knopf.
Adichie, Chimamanda Ngozi. 2014. "Americanah Author Explains Learning to Be Black in the US." *NPR*. http://www.npr.org/2014/03/07/286903648/americanah-author-explains-learning-to-be-black-in-the-u-s

Angelou, Maya. 1969. *I Know Why the Caged Bird Sings*. New York: Random House.
Archer, O. Jermaine. 2006. "Bitter Herbs and a Lock of Hair: Recollections of Africa in Slave Narratives of the Garrisonian Era." *Diasporic Africa: A Reader*, edited by Michael A. Gomez. New York and London: New York University Press.
Boyce-Davies, Carol. 1994. *Black Women Writing and Identity: Migrations of the Subject*. London and New York: Routeledge.
Bracks, Lean'tin L. 1998. *Writings on Black Women of the Diaspora: History, Language and Identity*. New York: Garland Publishing, Inc.
Campbell, Emory S. 2011. "Gullah Geechee Culture: Respected, Understood and Striving: Sixty Years After Lorenzo Dow Turner's Masterpiece, Africanisms in the Gullah Dialect." *The Black Scholar, The Living legend of Lorenzo Dow Turner: The First African American Linguist*, Vol. 41, No. 1 (Spring 2011), 77–84.
Douglass, Frederick. 2002. "Narrative of the Life of Frederick Douglass." *Classic Slave Narratives*, edited by Henry Louis Gates. New York: Signet.
Gyasi, Yaa. 2016. *Homegoing: A Novel*. New York: Vintage Books.
Haley, Alex. 1976. *Roots: The Story of an American Family*. Doubleday: New York.
Halter, Marilyn, and Violet Showers-Johnson. 2014. *African and American: West Africans in Post-Civil Rights America*. New York and London: New York University Press.
Hansberry, Lorraine. 1959. *A Raisin in the Sun*. New York: Random House.
Hines, Darlene Clark, William C. Hines, and Stanley Harold. 2008. *The African American Odyssey*. 4th Edition. New Jersey: Pearson and Prentiss Hall.
Jacobs, Harriet. 2002. "Incidents in the Life of a Slave Girl, 1861." *Classic Slave Narratives*, edited by Henry Louis Gates. New York: Signet.
Levine, Amy K. 2003. *Africanism and Authenticity in African American Women's Novels*. Gainesville: University Press of Florida.
Naylor, Gloria. 1998. *Mama Day*. New York: Knopf Doubleday.
Olaudah, Equiano. 1789. *The Interesting Life of Olaudah Equiano*. New York: Penguin Classics.
Prince, Mary. 2002. "A History of a West Indian Slave." *Classic Slave Narratives*, edited by Henry Louis Gates. New York: Signet.
Putzi, Jennifer. 2004. "Raising the Stigma": Black Womanhood and the Marked Body in Pauline Hopkins "Contending Forces." *College Literature*, Vol. 31, No. 2 (Spring 2004), 1–21.
Topke, Alvaroand Angel Serrano. 1998. *The Language You Cry In*. Documentary.

Chapter 2

Malian Immigration in France
Perspectives from African Women Writers of French Expression

Cheryl Toman

Until the end of the 1950s, the sub-Saharan African population in France consisted generally of members of an elite class mainly from Cameroon, Senegal, and Côte-d'Ivoire who were either commissioned to work for the French government or who had come to pursue their studies at schools and universities in Paris. Early literary works describing the African immigrant experience in France usually originated from this elite group, and these pioneering writers were overwhelmingly male. The production of literature by African Francophone women who aspired to be published faced many obstacles trying to get their works in print. Two examples of novels from this period that present a first glimpse of an African immigrant experience in Paris include Ivorian author Bernard Dadié's *Un nègre à Paris* (*An African in Paris*) written between 1956 and 1959 and Cameroonian writer Thérèse Kuoh-Moukoury's *Rencontres essentielles* (*Essential Encounters*), a novel actually completed in 1956 but not published until 1969.

Yambo Ouologuem, one of Mali's earliest novelists, was inspired to write a collection of essays he titled *Lettre à la France Nègre* "Letter to Black France" (1959), undoubtedly influenced by the period he spent in France for his studies. But Malian women writers were all but absent in Francophone literature until 1975 when Aoua Kéita published her 400-page autobiography titled *Femme d'Afrique: la vie d'Aoua Kéita racontée par elle-même* "Woman from Africa: the life of Aoua Kéita in her own words" (1975), considered a classic of African Francophone literature since it is the only published account of the precolonial period written by a Malian woman. However, Kéita spoke of her work as a midwife and an anticolonial activist mainly in Bamako, Gao, and Dakar as she did not study in France. Literary perspectives from a Malian woman writer on diaspora experiences in France would not appear until decades later. Few works of African Francophone literature exist, in fact, that trace Malian migration, and two of those are the specific focus of this chapter. Calixthe Beyala's *Loukoum: The "Little Prince" of Belleville* (1992) and Fatimata Diallo's *Sous mon voile* "Under my veil" (2015) are narratives about Malian immigration told from feminine and feminist perspectives in particular. Such authentic glimpses of Malian women are rare and furthermore, these writings stand out for their ability to capture two pivotal periods in Malian immigration history in France—the 1990s and the most recent times we are living today.

During the post–World War II construction boom in France, the French government invited foreign workers to apply for manual labor jobs, and the majority of Malians who took advantage of these early opportunities were men from the impoverished western region known as Kayes. Nearly all of these workers had left their families behind in Mali. A steady flow of Malians continued to arrive throughout the 1960s up until 1974 when a formal restriction of migrant labor in France was established (Trauner, 2005: 222). Four years later, however, in 1978, France's highest administrative court "recognized the right to a normal family as a fundamental constitutional right," thereby annulling an earlier restriction that interfered with a resident alien's right to be joined by a spouse or minor child (Guendelsberger, 1988: 3). Such family reunification laws led to a significant increase in Malian women in France; however, since almost all, at first, were spouses of migrant workers already in place, the stereotype emerged of the dependent and subservient Malian wife (Trauner, 2005: 223) with a brood of children to care for.

Unfortunately, this stereotype persists, despite the fact that Malian women in France today, for the most part, are far from passive. Prominent organizations run by and for Malian women in France such as the Association des Femmes Maliennes de Montreuil and the Fédération des Femmes Maliennes de France are renowned for their activism, organizing, and participating in community-building events, activities, and initiatives.

But the mere fact that French society has maintained these stereotypes from the early 1990s demonstrates how the efforts of Malians to integrate and assimilate are often ignored. In *Que vivent les femmes d'Afrique*, Tanella Boni points out that the incessant and open debate in France today on what qualifies one as "French" has pushed those who feel discriminated against to seek refuge in their communities where they can diminish the effects of living life as a "visible minority" (2011: 95). According to Boni's analysis, Malian women immigrants are subject to being placed in two adverse classifications in French society, as both Africans and females.

Statistics prove, in fact, that the percentage of African women—not to mention Malian women—participating in the formal French labor market is clearly higher than the participation of immigrant women from other EU countries (Trauner, 2005: 228). Furthermore, since the 1990s, it must be noted that, contrary to the prevailing stereotypes, Malian women have increasingly immigrated to France on their own without husbands or other family members, either for economic reasons or to pursue their studies. These statistics, however, are rarely—if ever—cited in the many debates both public and private in France today on the heated subject of immigration law reform.

Negative perceptions are, in part, the reason that in the 1980s and 1990s, France's Pasqua laws were established, making it even more difficult for anyone from a developing country to migrate and settle in France. What was particularly unfair was the fact that many who had been considered legal before such laws were enacted had then become illegal at a time that coincided with the rise in 1972 of the far-right party known as the Front National (FN) of which the main actors, namely the Le Pen family, are still prominent today. Despite ultimately losing run-off presidential elections in both 2002 and 2017, FN candidates nonetheless have increasingly held significant positions in the French National Assembly and in the European Parliament and this has had a disastrous effect on immigration law. It is the continual tightening of the Pasqua laws, for example, requiring of immigrants more and more documents and formalities proving established financial resources and so-called adequate housing, that explains why only half of the estimated 120,000 Malian immigrants currently in France have attained legal status (McCormick and Rieussec, 2017). These numbers are likely to increase as the political unrest that has plagued Mali since 2012 has pushed out more Malians from their homeland. The global forces that drive immigration that in turn sparks resistance from the Western nations that receive migrants are many; topping the list are perhaps the growing inequality in incomes and human security (Castles, 2013: 122).

Kofman et al. (2004) suggest that granting the right to unify the family has traditionally been considered as promoting the integration of migrants into a host country and current discussions in France in particular cite "the alleged 'failure' of integration," with the "'migrant family' increasingly being seen as an obstacle to integration as a site of patriarchal relationships and illiberal practices" (1). In addition to these lingering perceptions, Malian immigrants in France were dealt a new blow when on January 9, 2015, Amédy Coulibaly, a French national of Malian origin who had never actually held Malian citizenship, murdered hostages in a Kosher supermarket on the edge of Paris. This act was linked to killings of the writers of *Charlie Hebdo* two days prior, allegedly provoked by the satirical paper's controversial depiction of the Prophet Mohammed. One of the consequences of these tragic events was a fresh suspicion of Malians in France, as if Coulibaly had been a typical product of that community.

Admittedly, Western media accounts tend to fuel prejudice against immigrant communities and are thus not ideal sources for understanding the complex issues and personal stories surrounding immigration. Perhaps this is why over the last 25 years, there have been many examples of *migritude* literature in France—"migritude" being a fusion of "immigrant," or more accurately, the voice of the migrant, and *"négritude"*—a reference to the black literary movement of the late 1930s, 1940s, and 1950s, which had greatly changed the Paris literary scene, although women writers were conspicuously absent from it. The founders of *négritude* were said to have been inspired by the Harlem Renaissance of the 1920s and 1930s. In his essay, "Afrique(e)s-sur-Seine: autour de la notion de 'migritude,'" Jacques Chevrier (2004) claims that the *migritude* writer maintains a distance from the very two cultures that serve to define his or her identity, yet such a writer is ultimately inspired by being a product of both (96). These authors are thus writing from what Chevrier defines as a "third space" (2004: 99)—which may be a comfortable place or not—as we will see in the literary examples to follow. As a hybrid of two or more cultures, the writer enters into this third space, allowing him or her to examine and challenge the environment in which he or she lives. Dominic Thomas, author of *Black France: Colonialism, Immigration, and Transnationalism* describes such writing as a "process of mediation" (2006: 5).

But this process calls for feminine voices, which are too often missing or silenced. When looking at members of the Malian community who came to France after 1960 in particular, two texts of note by women writers come to mind: Beyala's *Loukoum: The "Little Prince" of Belleville* and Diallo's *Sous mon voile*, written 23 years apart. Beyala and Diallo not only provide readers with literary representations of more recent Malian immigrants to France, but they develop from a feminine if not feminist perspective further points of discussion such as polygamy and family, religious conservatism, and discrimination in schools and in the workplace. Most importantly, these texts give voices to the voiceless (or rather, they provide a platform for those whom others have refused to hear) and in the case of Diallo's autobiographical work, hers is a rare look at the immigrant experience using both raw emotion and careful analysis.

While one can say that these stories certainly provide a much-needed feminine perspective, the description "feminist" is used cautiously here, as to not give the impression that it is the Western ideology in play in this analysis. Many African writers and scholars have rejected the term outright (Oyěwùmi, 2003) or have qualified the term (Emecheta, 1988) because of what Juliana Makuchi Nfah-Abbenyi describes as "the neo-colonial tendencies that [they]see as intrinsic to feminism" (1997: 9). In her book, *Gender in African Women's Writing*, Nfah-Abbenyi also brings to the forefront African scholars who are "suspicious of a feminism that lays claim to radical separatist tendencies," because to them, it is important to "claim men as part of their struggle" (1997: 10).

This idea is exactly what motivated Beyala to coin her own term, *"féminitude,"* which she defines as being "very close to feminism but divergent in that it does not advocate for equality between men and women but recognizes instead that men and women are 'equally different'" (Beyala, 1995a: 20). Therefore, this analysis prefers an Afro-central definition of feminism as it was understood "before feminism became a movement with a global political agenda," as Nfah-Abbenyi explains, where "African women both 'theorized' and practiced what for them was crucial to the development of women, although no terminology was used to describe what these women were actively doing, and are still practicing on a day-to-day basis" (1997: 10).

One of the first literary perspectives of the Malian immigrant working class was made available not by a Malian surprisingly but rather by the Franco-Cameroonian author, Calixthe Beyala, and her 1992 novel, *Loukoum: Le "Petit Prince" de Belleville*. Set in the Paris neighborhood of Belleville, which straddles mainly the 11th and 20th districts of the city, the novel shows a vital African neighborhood before its residents were pushed out due to gentrification some years later. Although the story is fictional, Beyala had been living in Belleville at the time and had thus constructed her story based on actual people in the neighborhood. She recreated their experiences because she believed it was important to tell their stories. Furthermore, the text had been written at a time of dramatic change in immigration law in France. Although Beyala is not Malian, one cannot deny the significance of this work nonetheless, especially since novels by women writers from Mali did not appear until 1994 when Aïcha Fofana crafted *Mariage, on copie*. However, Fofana's novel is set in Bamako and not in France. Thus, Beyala's novel is one of the few representations of Malian immigrants from this transitional period in French society of the 1990s.

It is worthwhile to compare Beyala's work with an autobiography written more recently that is clearly considered an example of *migritude* literature. Fatimata Diallo's *Sous mon voile* was published in 2015 and provides a snapshot of the lives of Malians scattered today in the working-class suburbs of Paris just after the aforementioned January 2015 attacks. The backlash Malians encountered in France after those horrific events is central to the narrative.

An interesting fact about Diallo is that she had not contemplated writing her experiences until Pauline Peretz, an historian and editor of the literary collection associated with Pierre Rosanvallon's *Life Stories* project, approached her first and urged her to tell her story. Diallo's final product very much aligned with Rosanvallon's mission to publish texts that would create the equivalent of a "Parliament of Invisibles" that could play a role in remedying under-representation currently undermining democracy in France (2014: 11). Diallo had come to Paris in 2013 bursting with excitement to live in the French capital she had dreamed of. Yet, the reality of the 2-year period dedicated to her studies at the suburban campus of the University of Paris system known as Villetanneuse was much different (Peretz, 2016: 122). Diallo was earning her living as a sitter for the children of Peretz's friends, creating the opportunity for the two to meet. With Peretz's encouragement and guidance, Diallo told her story—orally at first and then arriving at a final written version only after sifting through transcripts and notes with Peretz. Just a few weeks after finishing, however, Diallo decided to return to Bamako to rejoin her family for good (Peretz, 2016: 122).

If we consider Beyala's and Diallo's texts together, we note that some of the same challenges facing the Malian community in France have remained throughout the years, but the growing acceptability of right-wing politics in French society along with new sources of tension have now further complicated the lives of Malian youth and their families in France. Although Beyala and Diallo have written their texts using vastly different approaches, both works help readers to understand the immigrant experience through the eyes of those who have lived it in these spaces, according to Eileen Julian, "where protagonists are challenged nonetheless by the racial and ideological histories and dynamics of the 'host country'" (2015: 23).

Loukoum: The "Little Prince" of Belleville is a story perceived through the eyes of Loukoum, a 10-year old Malian boy. His father, Abdou, is a sanitation worker and a French army veteran. In their home are three other children and two co-wives, M'am and Soumana, neither of whom are Loukoum's biological mother, but he refers to them as his two "mums," which irks his French schoolteachers to no end. This particular novel is among the first works to point out the racist and discriminatory policies of the French government concerning the composition of families. It also depicts the day-to-day existence of the Malian community and what they endure in the name of the values of the French republic. The lives of Malian subjects are shaped by the pressure of political realities so that immigrants have slowly morphed to conform, to some extent, to the desires of the growing right wing in France. Abdou and his family are not rebel rousers; they are hard-working, inconspicuous individuals striving to get by on the little income that they have, supplemented by government subsidies available to all French citizens and legal residents. By the end of the novel, however, Abdou is arrested after having been turned in by a social worker. He is accused of registering children in the social security system just to gain extra family benefits. The alleged story is far from the truth; what does happen, however, is that Abdou's two wives must secretly share one identity card in order to have access to health care since the French government does not officially recognize more than one wife per family (56).

It must be pointed out, however, that French society considers health care for all to be a fundamental human right so the fact that the two co-wives at one time share a benefits card speaks more to the hypocrisy of French society and to the anti-immigrant sentiment that prevails than to the dishonesty of the family. Tragically, the co-wife without official papers dies of a pulmonary embolism after she is too afraid to present her co-wife's identity card at the hospital in a last attempt to gain access to treatment (Beyala, 1995b: 115). The family's ordeal and the stereotypes and prejudice that plague them seem typical in the Malian diaspora. Moreover, knowledge of the background of immigrant problems and legal barriers and constraints in France at the time makes this story even more disturbing and thus Beyala's novel achieves its purpose of exposing French society's numerous contradictions.

Mali has always been a country with consistently high rates of polygamy. In 2015, statistics showed that overall, 41.8 percent of Malian women were in polygamous marriages (Dissa, 2016: 99) with the region of Kayes, from where the majority of Malian migrants post-1960 have come, being at a significantly higher rate of 51.8 percent (101). When Malians first immigrated to France, information about marital status had been readily disclosed by families and documented as such by French authorities since there were seemingly no repercussions for doing so. Between 1976 and 1993, the marital status of Malians in polygamous marriages was recognized and tolerated by the French government, although medical benefits and maternity leave were extended only to the first wife. All children, on the other hand, regardless of their biological mother, were given access to healthcare and this is exactly what plays out in Beyala's novel. In 1993, 1 year after the work was published, France officially prohibited polygamy as grounds for family reunification (Sargent and Cordell, 2003: 1963), and in some cases, it was justification for the confiscation of one's residence card or even for deportation. This meant that Malian families who had been legal residents for years had become "illegal" overnight in the eyes of the law.

However, legal battles were not the only source of worry for Malians who were widely ostracized for having large families at a time when, ironically, France was doing everything possible to raise the birthrate in the country. While the French government introduced countless pro-natalist incentives including tax breaks, generous family allocations, and employment benefits, non-European immigrants were openly excluded from such policies and, in fact, anti-natalist policies targeting immigrant families were put into place. These policies took a toll on countless individuals who were sought out and even harassed by social workers and family planning personnel each time they were encountered in schools and medical facilities. This is clearly the motivation behind Beyala's creation of the social worker in the novel, Madame Saddock, who relentlessly pursues Abdou's wives and children, lurking outside of their home to accost them once she is assured that Abdou has left for work (Beyala, 1995b: 79). Madame Saddock is the epitome of the *Franco-Française* (someone who considers herself "purely French") who tries to "rescue" African women and children from the oppressive African male authority figure, her vision clouded by racist views and stereotypes of African families.

One would be hard-pressed to find a more honest representation of this period than Beyala's novel. While the principal narrator is the boy, Loukoum, chapters start with poetic reflections, constructed as letters, from the eyes of his father, Abdou. In fact, there are passages that are incredibly insightful such as Abdou's letter to then French president François Mitterrand, warning of the dangers of the Le Pen family and asking him to ensure that the "vile plan" to run all the Malians out of France would not become a reality (Beyala, 1995b: 13). Abdou tells readers: "I would like very much to tell you about my country in a way that is different from what you've read in books. I know that you won't believe me" (Beyala, 1995b: 78). And also, "I have done nothing wrong, it's your legislation that has not integrated my customs" (Beyala, 1995b: 167). But perhaps the most poignant excerpt is one that acknowledges the divide in French society that has little chance of being mended, even today:

> I've immigrated. I've crossed frontiers. I've left fingerprints behind, and, on every occasion, a shred of flesh, a bit of my soul. Yes, friend, you, you who meet me every morning and cross your everyday words with my barren syllables—you who turn your head when my eyes stare at you and come with a thousand little questions to put on your forehead—you who look away when my lips struggle, mumbling words whose foreignness dismantles your weariness and fills you with a thousand spangles—you, over there, who seem affected by nothing—you, too, you annihilate me with your silence and beat me up whenever the desire takes you . . . listen. (Beyala, 1995b: 29)

The reader does, in fact, listen to the voices of Beyala's characters but as a woman writer, however, Beyala does not always let Abdou off the hook. Little Loukoum at age 10 already reiterates all that he has learned from his father about women: that they are nothing without men (Beyala, 1995b: 26), that men should not have any regard for what women say (32), that some are "whores," and that in France, the "grand women's revolution" has been "a natural disaster among the immigrants" (79). Although the reader sees Abdou's faults, the novel begins strategically with Abdou claiming how hard it is to lend his son to authorities other than his own (Beyala, 1995b:

1)—teachers, social workers, doctors, and others who ultimately do not respect him. These feelings, too, are perfectly understandable, especially when the reader sees the devastating effects of prejudice on the Malian community in French society. In an almost unbelievable move, Loukoum's teachers declare the boy illiterate in his school records even though he proves to them that he can read and write Quranic Arabic (Beyala, 1995b: 3).

The reader must not forget that the very generation of which Beyala speaks in this novel have now grown up and many surely have small children of their own and it is not difficult to see the roots of the anger of today's youth in France: they are products of this immigrant community who have been caught between two oppressive sources of authority in a sense. On the one hand, their immigrant parents have sometimes transmitted negative impressions of France based on their own experiences as both children and adults. On the other, these young people have encountered few if anyone in French society who will accept Malians or any other non-European immigrant as equals, let alone as true French citizens.

It is with these unfortunate realities in mind that we move to Fatimata Diallo's account of her recent immigrant experience as conveyed in her work, *Sous mon voile*. Similar to Beyala's novel, much of what Diallo experiences is a logical outcome of the discriminatory policies and racist attitudes of French society generated over the last 20 years.

Diallo's narrative begins in Bamako as she makes her decision to leave her home for Paris in order to pursue advanced studies, despite discouragement from friends and family (2015: 8). She has personally known many individuals who have migrated to France and who do not return to Mali and for her, this is proof that she is making the right decision. In Mali, Diallo has never felt constrained in terms of her personal freedom, but upon her arrival in France, she is entrusted to her father's friend who feels it is his duty to monitor her every move (2015: 11). What is more disconcerting to her is that he does nothing to integrate her into the family; she feels that she has little independence compared to her life in Mali and she is surprised by all the measures of security in France that restrict free movement. She is overwhelmed by bureaucracy and the reader gains insight into the impact of tightened immigration laws on gaining legal status in France. Diallo also experiences solitude that she has never known before. It is this extreme alienation coupled with other frustrations which transform her over time. In Mali, she was surrounded by family and friends, had a boyfriend, and often went out to clubs, played basketball, and dressed in Western-style clothing (Diallo, 2015: 17). In France, she develops a mistrust of anyone who is not related to her. And since she feels no one is close by to truly protect her, the veil becomes the means of protection she feels is missing. I do use the term "veil" here as opposed to *"hijab"* because of its occurrence in Diallo's title and throughout the text. Diallo becomes more conservative in the way she practices Islam: she only eats *halal*, she prays at all required times even if she must leave her lectures at the university to do so, and she refuses to shake hands with men (2015: 27).

In her spare time, she frequently consults Internet sites about the Quran and its interpretation and watches videos made by conservative Muslim clerics (Diallo, 2015: 20). But one cannot say that she has become radicalized—at no point does she entertain the thought of violence—although some French readers of her work may see this differently. But when read carefully, even those critical of Diallo's culture and beliefs are made to reassess the situation, a reaction provoked by words such as these: "Thanks to the veil, I wanted to protect myself. I wanted to be respected. I didn't know that my experience with France would be the opposite of what I thought and that I was going to feel such a strong hostility" (Diallo, 2015: 20). Diallo, in fact, must work hard to avoid letting bitterness get the best of her. She further explains:

> Since the January 2015 attacks, people look at me more than ever. They are constantly staring me down. I can tell it's my veil that is the cause of this. I feel such strong tension in the street, in the subway. When I get on the train, I feel that no one trusts me as if I was going to commit a terrorist act, as if I were a criminal. [. . .] Now when I enter the train, I look straight ahead, and as soon as I can, I close my eyes and I put in my ear buds to isolate myself and meditate. I pretend I'm sleeping; I don't want to see others staring at me. I don't want to feel such hostility. I'm afraid of feeling anger rising up in me. I keep myself together by thinking it won't always be like this, but I can't be sure. (Diallo, 2015: 31)

Ironically, her choices make her unhappier. Her father's friend is furious at her decision to veil and he retracts all offers to help her, including recommending her for employment. He tells her: "This is neither the time nor the place" (Diallo, 2015: 21), informing her that he would have understood if she had come to Paris veiled in the first place. Back in Bamako, her mother worries about her daughter's transformation and tells her she fears she would not even recognize her upon her return.

Diallo's decision to veil does make her life in France infinitely more difficult on many levels. In France, the veil is not allowed in elementary, middle, or high schools, but it is permitted on university campuses for the simple reason that university students are no longer minors and are considered free to make their own decisions on this matter (Body-Gendrot, 2007: 294). This does not mean, however, that wearing the veil on campus is socially accepted. Diallo's autobiography confirms reports that one commonly hears that students wearing a veil will feel uncomfortable in their own classrooms on French campuses, and at times, are intimidated or taunted by their own professors. French law also prohibits government employees from wearing the veil at work, but other types of employers are not allowed to discriminate against those who do. Nonetheless, this, too, is a problem for Diallo as she seeks employment. It is customary in France for a job candidate to add a photo to his or her CV and Diallo complains that this in addition to her Malian name are more than enough to cause her CV to be discarded by potential employers (2015: 88). In the end, Diallo decides to leave France and to consider studies in countries more accepting of the veil: The United States, the United Kingdom, Canada, or even Saudi Arabia (2015: 91–92). Diallo comes to much the same conclusion as Abdou does in Beyala's *Loukoum: The "Little Prince" of Belleville*—that she has done nothing wrong and that it is actually French law that has double standards in its application. And once again, this time in Diallo's work written over two decades after Beyala's novel, the contradiction in French society is cited—that France's core beliefs, "liberté, égalité, fraternité," do not apply to all. Diallo explains:

> One day, [a friend] asked me if I realized that because of my transformation, I had to give up the dream that I had in coming here—obviously, she was referring to the veil. She didn't understand when I told her it wasn't quite like that. For me, the problem isn't my veil, but France. Every day, I think about leaving here. "France, the country of freedom"—I no longer believe this. [. . .] As long as this country doesn't show tolerance with regards to women choosing to veil, I will always picture it as a hostile place. I'm determined to leave. (Diallo, 2015: 91)

Although African authors have been writing about immigration to France since the late 1950s, women's voices did not emerge until much later. The story of Malian immigrants is long and complex and works like Beyala's *Loukoum: The "Little Prince" of Belleville* and Diallo's *Sous mon voile* fill a void and give readers a more accurate and complete picture of their journey thus far. These two women writers have reiterated many of the sentiments that their male counterparts have expressed throughout the years but they have also brought to the forefront issues that concern immigrant women from Mali in particular, realities that had yet to be told from a feminine and/or feminist perspective. Many Africanist scholars over the years have pointed out the necessity for African women to write. Pius Adesanmi laments the fact that African literature early on was "an entirely male affair" (2004: 233). Juliana Makuchi Nfah-Abbenyi speaks famously of what she calls "the neglect of African women's writing" (1997): "What happened more often than not was that men—male writers, male critics—promoted their work and the ideas of other men such that even those images of women that were fostered systemically excluded images of women by women" (3).

Women do write differently from men and their contributions allow for a broader conversation. As Nfah-Abbenyi (1997) rightfully points out: "women are now writing about women and bringing not only their points of view but lived experiences as women to their writing (6). Over the last 27 years, Beyala's novel was met with great critical acclaim and in fact, is part of a trilogy about the same family that gave Beyala, in part, her renown as a Francophone writer. Diallo, too, managed to attract a very prominent publisher for her work thanks to the *Life Stories* project in France but it is still a bit too early to assess the book's critical success. The text itself probably could have benefitted from a preface or introduction as some readers may perceive Diallo's transformation as a radicalization of sorts. This is especially true in our post-911, post-*Charlie Hebdo* world in which the Western reader of an autobiography by an African Muslim woman "takes on the aspect of voyeur more than concerned humanitarian" (Bush, 2016: 130). But Diallo's book, like Beyala's work, explains at the very least how seeds of anger and erosion of identity have led a few of immigrant origin in this unfortunate direction of radicalization.

Although these works focus on individuals of the Malian diaspora, the experiences depicted are not unlike those of other non-European immigrants in France and in other Western countries and readers are made even more aware of issues that still need to be addressed such as questionable immigration policies that have been hastily drafted as a response to rampant anti-immigrant sentiment. While unrest in Mali and the general threat of terrorism due to extremist groups in the north of the country since 2012 have brought yet another wave of Malian immigrants to France, their presence is less noticeable amidst the deluge of those arriving by boat to European shores from Syria, Libya, Central Asia, and other war-torn regions that have set up camps along the periphery of Paris and on the shores of Calais near the entrance to the Eurostar tunnel to Great Britain where many have convinced themselves that this is the best place to ask for political asylum.

But African women do have their own unique stories to tell that add to a conversation about the intersectionality of race, class, and gender and how each of these plays a role in determining an immigrant's quality of life and his or her ability to integrate and be accepted by the host society. These works by Beyala and Diallo are essential pieces of a collage of writings that provide a feminine perspective on Malian immigration to France; admittedly, these examples are few in literature with only one other prominent title on the subject that comes to mind, Nathalie Etoké's *Un amour sans papiers* "Undocumented love" (1999), the story of a Cameroonian student in France who meets and falls in love with an "illegal" immigrant from Mali who is eventually deported. These three texts exist within a still larger body of work focusing on African immigration to Europe that include francophone novels by prominent Senegalese women writers like Aminata Sow Fall and more recently, Fatou Diome. Fall's novel, *Douceurs du bercail* (1998) "Sweetness of home," tells of a young Senegalese female journalist on assignment in France whose reaction to the unwarranted harassment by a customs officer lands her in the airport's detention center for a prolonged stay. Diome's *Celles qui attendent* (2010) "Waiting women" is a work comprised of four intertwining survival stories of the lives of wives and mothers of clandestine migrants who have set off for Europe. Diome provides a rare look at the families left behind—with a focus on female members of those families—who suffer not only from fewer available economic resources but also from the constant stress of being without any news on the well-being of their loved ones abroad.

The power of each of these aforementioned literary works has thus proven to be greater than media sources in terms of alerting the public about the realities that immigrants experience, reminding readers that immigration is not only about numbers and statistics but about human beings. Belleville's Malian community has since relocated to the Parisian suburb of Montreuil and elsewhere. Calixthe Beyala has moved on to entirely new subjects in her writings and unfortunately there is no indication that Fatimata Diallo will continue as a writer. But the creative artistry of African diaspora women writers produces powerful writings that narrate the experience of Malian and other African immigrants in Western spaces through the lens of gender. In the context of African oral traditions, contemporary Malian music by female artists such as Inna Modja, Fatoumata Diawara, and the legendary Oumou Sangaré speaks to these issues. Malian women artists today are contemporary storytellers expressing the realities of life in the diaspora, performing without the required initiation typical for traditional griots who for centuries have been storytellers, musicians, poets, and historians all in one. These writers and artists from Mali represent just one piece of a complicated puzzle that tells the story of African immigration to France, from past to present.

REFERENCES

Adesanmi, Pius. 2004. "Of Postcolonial Entanglement and Durée: Reflections on the Francophone African Novel." *Comparative Literature* 56, no. 3 (Summer): 227–242.

Beyala, Calixthe. 1992. *Le petit prince de Belleville*. Paris: Albin Michel.

Beyala, Calixthe. 1995a. *Lettre d'une Africaine à ses sœurs occidentales*. Paris: Spengler.

Beyala, Calixthe. 1995b. *Loukoum: The "Little Prince" of Belleville*. Translated by Marjolijn de Jager. Portsmouth: Heinemann.

Body-Gendrot, Sophie. 2007. "France Upside Down Over a Headscarf?" *Sociology of Religion* 68, no. 3 (Fall): 289–304.

Boni, Tanella. 2011. *Que vivent les femmes d'Afrique?* Paris: Karthala.

Bush, Glen. 2015. "Survivalist Autobiographies: The Struggles of African Muslim Women." In *The Critical Imagination in African Literature: Essays in Honor of Michael J.C. Echeruo*, edited by Maik Nwosu Obiwu, 129–152. Syracuse: Syracuse University Press.

Castles, Stephen. 2013. "The Forces Driving Global Migration." *Journal of Intercultural Studies* 34, no. 2: 122–140.

Chevrier, Jacques. 2004. "Afrique(s)-sur-Seine: Autour de la notion de 'migritude.'" *Notre Librairie* 155–156 (July–Dec): 96–100.

Dadié, Bernard. 1959. *Un Nègre à Paris*. Paris: Présence Africaine.

Diallo, Fatimata. 2015. *Sous mon voile*. Paris: Seuil.

Diome, Fatou. 2010. *Celles qui attendent*. Paris: Flammarion.

Dissa, Yaya. 2016. "Polygamy in Mali: Social and Economic Implications on Families." *International Journal of African and Asian Studies* 27: 99–108.

Ekotto, Frieda, and Ken Harrow, eds. 2015. *Rethinking African Cultural Production*. Bloomington: Indiana University Press.

Emecheta, Buchi. 1988. "Feminism with a Small 'f'!" In *Criticism and Ideology*, edited by Kirsten Holst Peterson, 173–185. Uppsala: Scandinavian Institute of African Studies.

Etoké, Nathalie. 1999. *Un amour sans papiers*. Paris: Cultures Croisées.

Fall, Aminata Sow. 1998. *Douceurs du bercail*. Abidjan: Nouvelles Editions Ivoiriennes.

Fofana, Aïcha. 1994. *Mariage, on copie*. Bamako: Jamana.

Guendelsberger, John. 1988. "The Right to Family Unification in French and United States Immigration Law." *Cornell International Law Journal* 21, no. 1: 2–101.

Julian, Eileen. 2015. "The Critical Present: Where is 'African Literature'?" In *Rethinking African Cultural Production*, edited by Frieda Ekotto and Ken Harrow, 17–28. Bloomington: Indiana University Press.

Kéita, Aoua. 1975. *Femme d'Afrique: La vie d'Aoua Kéita racontée par elle-même*. Paris: Présence Africaine.

Kofman, Eleonore, Madalina Rogoz, and Florence Lévy. 2010. "Family Migration Policies in France." In *International Centre for Migration Policy Development Working Papers Series*, 1–34. Vienna: ICMPD.

Kuch-Moukoury, Therese. 2002. *Essential Encounters*. Translated by Cheryl Toman. New York: MLA Texts and Translations Series.

Kuoh-Moukoury, Thérèse. 1969. *Rencontres essentielles*. Paris: Adamawa.

McCormick, Ty, and Sebastian Rieussec. 2017. "The Deported." *The Pulitzer Center Online*, October 4, 2017. http://pulitzercenter.org/reporting/deported-bamako.

Nfah-Abbenyi, Juliana Makuchi. 1997. *Gender in African Women's Writing: Identity, Sexuality, and Difference*. Bloomington: Indiana University Press.

Obiwu, Maik Nwosu, ed. 2015. *The Critical Imagination in African Literature: Essays in Honor of Michael J.C. Echeruo*. Syracuse: Syracuse University Press.

Ouologuem, Yambo. 1959. *Lettre à la France Nègre*. Paris: Le Serpent à Plumes.

Oyěwùmi, Oyèrónké, ed. 2003. *African Women & Feminism: Reflecting on the Politics of Sisterhood*. Trenton: Africa World Press.

Peretz, Pauline. 2016. "Écrire pour autrui." *Le sujet dans la cité* 7 (November): 121–127.

Petersen, Kirsten Holst, ed. 1988. *Criticism and Ideology*. Uppsala: Scandinavian Institute of African Studies.

Rabaka, Reiland. 2016. *The Negritude Movement: W.E.B. Du Bois, Leon Damas, Aime Cesaire, Leopold Senghor, Frantz Fanon, and the Evolution of an Insurgent Idea*. Lanham: Lexington Books.

Rosanvallon, Pierre. 2014. *Le parlement des invisibles*. Paris: Seuil.

Sargent, Carolyn, and Dennis Cordell. 2003. "Polygamy, Disrupted Reproduction, and the State: Malian Migrants in Paris, France." *Social Science & Medicine* 56: 1961–1972.

Thomas, Dominic. 2006. *Black France: Colonialism, Immigration, and Transnationalism*. Bloomington: Indiana University Press.

Trauner, Helene. 2005. "Dimensions of West African Immigration to France: Malian Immigrant Women in Paris." *Stichproben: Vienna Journal of African Studies* 5, no. 8: 221–235.

Chapter 3

Waithood and Girlhood in NoViolet Bulawayo's *We Need New Names*

Amanda Lagji

NoViolet Bulawayo's 2013 novel *We Need New Names* follows the protagonist Darling as she transitions from childhood in rural Zimbabwe to adolescence in America, mapping the spatiotemporal locus of coming-of-age and her diasporic movement through space. Much like classic bildungsromane, where the maturation journey involves autonomy, economic stability, and successful integration into society, Darling expects that movement to America will entail progress, economic mobility, and increased security as she embraces new locations and cultures. This chapter argues that *We Need New Names* troubles the teleology of future-oriented bildungsromane by dwelling in the temporality of waiting and can be productively read as a literary examination of contemporary "waithood."

Rather than merely a sign of disillusionment, the temporal constraints of Darling's waithood encourage her to create new social connections that, if not successful in achieving the incorporation of traditional bildungsromane, do prompt her to develop strategies to give shape and meaning to the vagaries of waiting. Bulawayo's novel exhibits the characteristics of suspension and liminality similar to those identified by ethnographic studies of youth in the global South. This waiting, while certainly signaling disappointment and disillusionment, is not utterly disempowering; instead, Darling quite literally takes aim at the timings and tempos of coming-of-age expectations—on the personal and national level—as well as at the generic conventions of the linear, future-oriented classic bildungsroman.

The concept of waithood captures a crisis in the rites of passage that have traditionally marked transitions between youth and adulthood, and this crisis is evident throughout postcolonial bildungsromane such as *We Need New Names*. Drawing from the concept of waithood, and departing from Joseph Slaughter's important work on human rights discourses and the bildungsroman, this chapter examines the way that the deferral of incorporation in *We Need New Names* not only strongly indicts Zimbabwe's government and larger global flows of capital and power but also revises the connotations of disillusionment—passivity and disempowerment—through the temporality of waiting. Thus, this chapter argues that the association of girlhood and waithood in Bulawayo's novel centers the temporality of waiting in Darling's diasporic experience, positing waiting as a critical temporal modality to challenge the assumptions of modernity, progress, and development that undergird other bildungsromane.

One of the most influential accounts of bildungsromane in postcolonial contexts is Joseph Slaughter's *Human Rights Inc.* (2007), which argues that the genre "provided the dominant novelistic form for depicting and acquiring this new national and historical consciousness," on which human rights discourses also depend (31). A bildungsroman, according to Slaughter, is "the didactic story of an individual who is socialized in the process of learning for oneself what everyone else (including the reader) presumably already knows" (2007: 3). The integration and self-fulfillment that characterize a traditional bildungsroman, however, are absent in the postcolonial variety, which "narrates the failure of incorporation and the corruption of the democratic egalitarian imaginary" (Slaughter, 2007: 135). Instead, the incorporation that links both discourses of human rights and the bildungsroman remains "a vanishing (plot) point beyond the frame of the text" (Slaughter, 2007: 215). These "transformations of the *Bildungsroman*'s normative generic conventions," Slaughter writes, "problematize the assumption of the 'irrepressible march of freedom and human rights,' because these novels exhibit the 'current state' of human rights discourse's 'still-unfulfilled promise, of their "tradition of what has not yet become"'" (2007: 39).

Strikingly, Slaughter's own account of human rights discourse embeds the temporality of waiting already: he writes that "contemporary human rights is largely a proleptic discourse and law governing a future universalism, *awaiting* actualization." (2007: 84, emphasis mine). Under this configuration, waiting indexes disillusionment; a character who is still waiting for incorporation, or a country waiting for the promises of independence to be realized, are the hallmarks of the disillusionment genre of postcolonial writing after the exultant, early 1960s. However, the temporality of "waiting" does different work in *We Need New Names* through the instantiation of waithood. Waithood, as the following discussion will show, does not necessarily, or only, insinuate disillusionment or failure.

The term waithood emerges as a term that can both capture the prevalence of the temporalities of waiting across the global South, *and* pry apart the intuitive association of waiting with passivity and disillusionment. Developed by scholars working in Middle Eastern and North African studies, the term "waithood" describes the circumstances of young people who "are increasingly unable to become social adults and full-fledged citizens" (Honwana, 2012: 4). According to Alcinda Honwana, who uses the term in her ethnographic study of youths in Tunisia, waithood describes a "period of prolonged adolescence or an involuntary delay in reaching adulthood, in which young people are unable to find employment, get married, and establish their own families" (2012: 4). Importantly, waithood is not a time of inactive waiting, but rather a period of dynamic creativity where "new forms of being and interacting with society" are created (Honwana, 2012: 4). This trend has been noted by scholars working all over the global South, from Craig Jeffrey's work on Indian youth (2010) to Adeline Masquelier's study of boredom and tea-making in Niger (2013), to Ato Quayson's analysis of gymming in Accra (2014), and Marc Sommers's book *Stuck: Rwandan Youth and the Struggle for Adulthood* (2012). Waithood troubles the expectation that youths will transition into conventional forms of adulthood; Honwana observes that "waithood is becoming a permanent condition, as many young people remain stuck in this in-between situation . . . a new but socially attenuated form of adulthood" (2012: 20). Despite their disparate geographies, these studies all involve contexts where waithood is linked tightly to economic stagnation, as youths are unable "to enter the labor market," and thereby "attain the social markers of adulthood" (Honwana, 2012: 19).

Economic stagnation is indeed signaled early in *We Need New Names*, as the children of the ironically named Paradise canvass the wealthier town Budapest, looking for guavas to fill their empty bellies. The children's circumstances are reflective of the economic crisis in Zimbabwe at the time of the novel's publication. The country's economy suffers from hyper-inflation and cash scarcity, leading to long lines at banks that Celia W. Dugger describes in a 2008 *New York Times* article resonantly titled "Life in Zimbabwe: Wait for Useless Money." Additionally, the government's 2005 "demolition and eviction campaign," Operation Murambatsvina, left an estimated 700,000 people homeless (Tibaijuka, 2005: 7). Darling recounts her first-hand experience of Operation Murambatsvina in a chapter titled "Real Change," explaining that she is afraid of the police and bulldozers because they razed the "real" home she used to live in (Bulawayo, 2013: 67). Darling remembers that "[w]hen the bulldozers finally leave, everything is broken, everything is smashed, everything is wreck" (Bulawayo, 2013: 68). The bulldozers are indiscriminate, leveling buildings and people, including one woman's home while her sleeping baby, named Freedom, was inside (Bulawayo, 2013: 69). Operation Murambatsvina, a 2005 UN report notes, was also called "'Operation Tsunami' because of its speed and ferocity" (Tibaijuka, 2005: 7), which Darling affirms when she remembers that adults cried, "It's like a tsunami tore through this place, Jesus, it's like a fucking tsunami tore this up" (Bulawayo, 2013: 69).

The children, bellies filled with guava, articulate their diasporic dreams, imagining new lives in America, Budapest, Johannesburg, or London. These dreams of economic mobility entail movements both upward and outward, but at a time Darling imagines further removed in the future. When Bastard remarks that they will eventually steal from inside of the houses, Darling thinks, "I'm not really worried about that because *when that time comes*, I'll not be here; I'll be living in America with Aunt Fostalina, eating real food and doing better things than stealing. *But for now*, the guavas" (Bulawayo, 2013: 12, emphasis mine). Later, when Darling brags that "it won't be long" until she goes to America to live, Bastard rejoins with a prescient warning: "What if you get there and find it's a kaka place and get stuck and can't come back? [. . .] you have to be able to return from wherever you go" (Bulawayo, 2013: 16). Although Darling posits a teleology of progress and improvement in a future movement from Zimbabwe to America, Bastard undermines her faith in ways that anticipate the novel's critique of the bildungsroman's promise of self-fulfillment and integration.

As a novel of formation and development, the bildungsroman traditionally focuses on a protagonist's growth and development, and concludes with his—indeed, earlier taxonomic approaches to describing the bildungsroman genre "exclude[d] female experience from the genre" (Boes, 2012: 234)—successful integration into society. Franco Moretti's seminal *The Way of the World: The Bildungsroman in European Culture* argues that the bildungsroman narrative is propelled forward by the protagonist's efforts to accomplish self-development and social integration, at which point the protagonist matures, "the narration has fulfilled its aim and can peacefully end" (1987: 18–19). But this integration in the *postcolonial* bildungsroman, according to Slaughter, is deferred beyond the novel's conclusion, and *We Need New Names* certainly does postpone Darling's transition to adulthood and her reconciliation with society alike. Waiting-as-postponement characterizes Darling's diasporic experiences from Africa to North America. Darling's hardships mirror Zimbabwe's postcolonial difficulties—not in an allegorical way, but through different scales of waiting.

Rather than viewing *We Need New Names* as a kind of anti-bildungsroman for its transgression of some of the classic characteristics of the genre, the novel as a coming-of-age story might instead be understood as illuminating the central contradictions embedded in the "classic'" form in the first place. Although Slaughter suggests that disillusionment is characteristic of the postcolonial bildungsroman specifically, other scholars find disillusionment present in European examples as well. Ralph Austen's "Struggling with the African Bildungsroman" notes, "Although postcolonial critics have often treated the European bildungsroman as a triumphalist assertion of individual modernity, students of this genre on its home grounds are less sanguine or unanimous about its ideological content" (2015: 220). Austen then goes on to identify four forms of bildungsromane, including the classical, disillusioned, optimistic, and the "'modernist' . . . return to disillusionment" (2015: 220). Although Austen concedes that "African bildungsromane address a different history than their European counterparts," he concludes that "they only enrich our understanding of the genre as well as Africa's place in the world" (2015: 228). This version of the postcolonial or African bildungsroman encourages scholars to resist positioning *We Need New Names* and other African bildungsromane as derivative of European forms, and to move away from positing the European tradition as a ruler against which to measure African iterations.

Although both the European and postcolonial variety may share disillusionment, the maturation journey in postcolonial and African bildungsromane tends to look different as the genre travels. The protagonist is not simply integrated into society and reconciled with its norms and contradictions but rather actively critiques society itself; a failure to integrate, for example, may index the impossibility of reconciling diametrically opposed desires and demands. *Nervous Conditions*, considered a classic African bildungsroman, is exemplar in this regard. *We Need New Names* has much in common with *Nervous Conditions* (1988), published by Zimbabwean writer Tsitsi Dangarembga. Discussion of African bildungsromane often turns to Dangarembga's seminal novel, which follows protagonist Tambu's transition from homestead to her uncle's home, concluding ambivalently with Tambu's acceptance to a majority-white and racially segregated all-girls school. *Nervous Conditions* is a retrospective narrative, and many critics have noted that the "crucial development stage, the moment of coming-of-age that the bildungsroman promises to put at the center of the narrative, is instead deferred into the narrative future" (Hay, 2013: 318).

There is great distance between the younger Tambu, who experiences the transition, and the older, wiser Tambu, who narrates and comments on the systemic oppression she witnessed, but the unification of these perspectives is not directly depicted in the text. Nevertheless, Tambu's story exhibits the "classic European elements of autonomous reading and mentorship" that make *Nervous Conditions* an important interlocutor for the story Bulawayo narrates (Austen, 2015: 219). Tambu is influenced by her cousin Nyasha, who struggles to reintegrate in Zimbabwe after spending years away in England as a young girl. As a result of Nyasha's mental breakdown and struggles with anorexia, coupled with her own experiences of oppression and prejudice, Tambu concludes her story with a gesture toward the struggles to come: "Quietly, unobstrusively and extremely fitfully, something in my mind began to assert itself, to question things and refuse to be brainwashed, bringing me to this time when I can set down this story" (Dangarembga, 2004: 208). Although how Tambu's development will proceed is not entirely clear by the novel's conclusion, Dangarembga clearly situates Tambu in assertive opposition to the situation in which she finds herself.

If critique and opposition are characteristic of the African bildungsroman, then additional links to other bildungsroman traditions become visible, such as to the African American bildungsroman or postcolonial bildungsromane set in other times and places. Rita Felski, for example, elucidates the contours of the feminist bildungsroman—a heading under which *Nervous Conditions*, and perhaps *We Need New Names* could be filed—which differs from the male bildungsroman in that "the journey into society does not signify a surrender of ideals and a recognition of limitations, but rather constitutes the precondition for oppositional activity and engagement" (1989: 137). Likewise, the African American bildungsroman, Gunilla Kester observes, depicts society as antagonistic or oppositional, whereas in "most other European *Bildungsromane* society is usually depicted as a benevolent force which envelopes the worthy individual with care" (1995: 9). Moreover, African American bildungsromane counter the "classical" form—which is usually "chronological, linear, third person" as well as "white, male, Western, and with a distinct positivistic bias"—with narratives that interrupt "the chronology of events" and "replace the notion of individuality with a collective, 'trans-individual subject'" (Kester, 1995: 17).

Both the disruption of linear chronology and the turn away from the individualistic focus of the "white, male, Western" bildungsroman are important characteristics of *We Need New Names*, and are conditions through which waithood emerges. Like other Zimbabwean novels that feature child narrators or protagonists, *We Need New Names* mobilizes childhood to "contest, disrupt, and threaten 'the lifespan of nationalist discourse' in Zimbabwe" (Muponde, 2015: 3). The phrase "*lifespan* of nationalist discourse" is particularly suggestive not only for fiction with child protagonists but also for postcolonial bildungsromane in which incorporation and self-realization appear postponed beyond the novel's final pages. In *Some Kinds of Childhood: Images of History and Resistance in Zimbabwean Literature* (2015), Robert Muponde notes that *We Need New Names* and other novels like it "useful[ly] interrup[t] . . . the maintenance of the accepted teleology along which the child is guided into expected adulthood by the adult" (142). Both the nation-state's sovereignty and the child's development are suspended or modified here. Bulawayo's novel does indeed depict a world where children are not only *not* guided into adulthood by adults but also a world where children give birth to children; the very first chapter, Hitting Budapest, introduces the main focalizing character, Darling, as well as her friend Chipo. Chipo is eleven, and pregnant—later, the text reveals that she has been raped by her grandfather. Darling comments that Chipo "used to outrun everybody in all of Paradise but not anymore because somebody made her pregnant" (Bulawayo, 2013: 4). From the beginning, *We Need New Names* disrupts the conventions of the bildungsroman as children parent other children, and Chipo's pregnancy threatens to stop her in her tracks. Chipo's development at the novel's opening seems paradoxically both arrested and accelerated, disrupting the "accepted teleology" described by Muponde, and indexing a change in the temporal apprehension and representation of becoming.

This temporal alteration can be best characterized as "waithood," and is shared by Chipo and the other children of Paradise, but most fully articulated in the narrative arc of Darling's character. This focus on waithood builds in part from Slaughter's analysis, whose discussion of postponement or suspension in postcolonial bildungsromane generally embeds the temporality of waiting. But reading *We Need New Names* in conjunction with waithood specifically departs from other analyses of the novel that focus predominantly on its representation of diasporic experiences primarily in terms of space, as opposed to time. These readings range from James Arnett's focus on photography and digital space (2016) to Isaac Ndlovu's study of migration and citizenship in the novel (2016). Camille Isaacs bridges these spatial foci by reading globalized existences through social media and cyberspace. Isaacs argues that Darling is both "adolescen[t] and migran[t]" whose "subjectivit[y] [is] located between the spaces of childhood and adulthood" (2016: 177). Quoting Homi Bhabha, she argues that "[t]hese 'in-between spaces' provide the terrain for elaborating strategies of selfhood" (2016: 177). Rather than repeating an interrogation of the *spaces* of transition, combining waithood with coming-of-age girlhood foregrounds the *times* of transition, or the *temporality* of transition in *We Need New Names*—especially the time of protracted waiting that seems to increasingly characterize adolescence for Darling and her peers.

Several characteristics of waithood, as described by Honwana—involuntary delay in achieving the social markers of adulthood, leading to a prolonged period poised between childhood and adulthood—are evident in the first chapter of *We Need New Names*. Chipo's pregnancy itself blurs the lines between childhood and adulthood and her refusal to speak underscores that her experiences cannot be narrated in conventional coming-of-age forms. Darling clarifies that Chipo is not "mute-mute; it's just that when her stomach started showing, she stopped talking" (Bulawayo, 2013: 4). Coupled with Chipo's inability to run as she used to, Chipo's pregnancy and immobility contrast sharply with Darling's dreams to live in America with "real" food and presumably a "real" childhood (Bulawayo, 2013: 12). Other details in the first chapter, especially the description of the unemployed parents of Darling and her friends, strengthen the association of Paradise with waithood. Although the children know that they ought not to leave Paradise, they also know that "the mothers are busy with hair and talk, which is the only thing they ever do" and the men "never lift [their eyes] from the draughts" (Bulawayo, 2013: 3–4). The unemployment and economic precariousness of Paradise give the children a preview of what their own futures might hold if they stay; the waithood that characterizes the lives of Darling's parents and the other adults signals an absence of the traditional markers of adulthood that would mark a clear transition out of childhood in that setting. Darling and her friends' designation of the products and settings that provide economic security as "real" (while the impoverished Paradise is, in contrast, "kaka") forge associations between realness, employment, money, and adulthood. As a result, becoming a "real" adulthood in Paradise seems to be postponed indefinitely.

In another deviation from the conventions of bildungsromane, which typically foreground the protagonist's educational journey as a conduit to formation or development, Darling and her friends have had their studies discontinued. This too is linked to Zimbabwe's economic crisis, as "all the teachers left to teach over in South Africa and Botswana and Namibia and them, where there's better money" (Bulawayo, 2013: 32–33). Bildungsromane in the European tradition tend to privilege autodidactic learning, such as the independent reading Jane Eyre engages at the beginning of her own coming-of-age story. Bulawayo draws clear connections to this bildungsroman convention in her own novel through Darling's reading habits. In *We Need New Names*, Yogita Goyal observes, Darling begins to read *Jane Eyre* (1847)—"the classic Bildungsroman of feminist self-consolidation"—but cannot finish it, citing Jane's "'stupid decisions' that bore her" (2017: 653). This refusal and inability to relate to Jane's story is significant in Darling's postcolonial, Zimbabwean setting. Ralph Austen notes that the "'unprescribed reading' and 'self-education'" of European bildungsromane "become especially acute in the African bildungsroman, where literacy itself is an issue inevitably associated with an alien colonial education system" (2015: 218). Darling, when she lives in her home country, is less conflicted about the imposition of English as such, and more concerned about the schools that have closed because the teachers have fled to bordering countries for work. Whereas earlier bildungsromane such as *Nervous Conditions* foregrounds the conflicts protagonists experience between different cultures and educational systems, *We Need New Names* expands the critique to incorporate the postcolonial Zimbabwean state for keeping the education she desires out of reach.

In the absence of formal schooling, the children spend their time playing the Country-Game, where they compete to be Western countries instead of "this one we live in—who wants to be a terrible place of hunger and things falling apart?" (Bulawayo, 2013: 43) and waiting for an NGO lorry to distribute goods in Paradise. Again mapping mobility onto desirability, Darling and her friends "are running away from North Korea" in the Country-Game when the lorry arrives (Bulawayo, 2013: 52). Immediately, the NGO workers discipline the children to wait in line, an orientation in time and space that arrests their movement and stifles the outward expression of desire and longing. Darling comments,

> What we really want to do is take off and run to meet the lorry but we know we cannot. Last time we did, the NGO people were not happy about it, like we had committed a crime against humanity. So now we just sing and wait for the lorry to approach us instead. The waiting is painful; we watch the lorry getting closer and closer, but it seems far away at the same time, like it's not even here yet but stuck somewhere else, in another country. It's the gifts that we know are inside that make it hard to wait and watch the lorry crawl. (Bulawayo, 2013: 53)

Darling's description emphasizes the tortured experience of prolonged waiting. Her hyperbole—"like we had committed a crime against humanity"—reveals the power of the NGO representatives to discipline the children into appropriate waiting, as well as to undercut the reasonableness of the request to wait. Darling additionally registers anxiety that the anticipated lorry will never arrive and remain "stuck somewhere else." This anxiety is heightened by the fact that the NGO truck is late this month (Bulawayo, 2013: 53). Although the lorry's arrival ostensibly brings an end to the children's waiting, the request to continue to wait in line lays bare the way time registers power and maps onto space; the three foreign white NGO workers are horrified by the children's pushing and screaming, and the gifts are distributed only after "[w]e stand in a neat line again and wait patiently" (Bulawayo, 2013: 57). In this way, the workers insist that Darling and her friends recognize that waiting is the appropriate response to foreign NGOs from the position of dispossession and poverty.

Waiting in line makes visible the power disparity between the white foreign workers and the inhabitants of Paradise, clearly demarcating those who have the power to force others to wait, and those who can only comply. The text strengthens this association of waiting with power by intimating the violence that inheres in and results from this disparity; the workers hand the children toy guns, and after the lorry departs, the children "take off and run to kill each other with our brand-new guns from America" (Bulawayo, 2013: 59). In addition to this violence that results from waiting, Bulawayo carefully identifies these "gifts" as originating in America, which is significant for the future that Darling anticipates will await her when she joins Aunt Fostalina. Just as Bastard warns that one should be careful to plan for a return so that one is not "stuck" elsewhere, here Bulawayo foreshadows Darling's arrival in America as one that will continue, rather than disrupt, the experiences of waiting and violence in Paradise.

Thus, *We Need New Names* expands waithood's economic critique to indict not only Zimbabwe, where limited opportunities encourage parents to cross-national borders to work in South Africa, but also America, the country in which Darling lives out her adolescence. This concern about waiting and the inability to return becomes a reality for Darling, who inadvertently becomes an undocumented immigrant in America. Her Aunt Fostalina explains that she cannot visit home for the time being because "you came on a visitor's visa, and that's expired; you get out, you kiss this America bye-bye" (Bulawayo, 2013: 191). The transition to security and selfhood Darling expects in America is jeopardized by this ambivalent status. As both citizen- and deportee-in-waiting, a phrase coined by Bridget Haas in "Citizens-in-Waiting, Deportees-in-Waiting: Power, Temporality, and Suffering in the U.S. Asylum System" (Haas, 2017: 75). Darling's experience is predominantly one of contingency and impermanence. Honwana notes that waithood captures the experience of children who neither become "social adults" nor "full-fledged" citizens (2012: 4), and in the novel's refusal to depict Darling transitioning to adulthood, embracing citizenship in Zimbabwe, or attaining permanent status in the United States, it appears that Darling's coming-of-age has been arrested and stalled in waithood.

However, according to Honwana, waithood ought not to be understood as a *failed* transition, which would reify the normative teleology of development that undergirds the transition to adulthood as well as to nationhood, but rather a new and difficult phase (Honwana, 2012: 37). Waithood, in this way, is distinguished from the arrested development that Jed Esty identifies in late 19th- and early twentieth-century bildungsromane in *Unseasonable Youth*. According to Esty, "the developmental logic of the late bildungsroman underwent substantial revision as the relatively stable temporal frames of national destiny gave way to a more conspicuously global, and therefore more uncertain, frame of social reference" (2012: 6). His study concerns youths who refuse to grow up or who age prematurely, and in this way "youth retains its grip on the center of the text, disorganizing and distending the plot" (2012: 18). Characterized as "modernist plots of stalled and/or accelerated *Bildung*," Esty suggests that these novels "expose modernity's temporal contradictions, particularly in zones of colonial encounter" (2012: 36). This examination of arrested development and growth is useful, insofar as it points to a correspondence between temporal critiques and form. But Darling's development is neither arrested nor stalled in waithood; waithood is an entirely new phase experienced by children, youths, and some adults alike, which forces a re-examination of the social and economic markers of adulthood and maturity. Temporalities of waithood and suspension have long been concerns of (post)colonial bildungsromane; Wangari wa Nyatetũ-Waigwa describes the "liminal novel" as one where the novel concludes before the rites of passage to adulthood are accomplished (1996: 3). Waithood is similar to liminality as Nyatetũ-Waigwa conceives of it because liminality is "a period of potentiality, spells not failure but suspension, and therefore it offers some remnants of hope" (Nyatetũ-Waigwa, 1996: 10).

To summarize thus far, *We Need New Names* shares with the classical bildungsroman a concern with the development and education of a young protagonist, and with later bildungsroman the mobilization of temporal disruption as a narrative strategy of critique. As Darling moves from Africa to North America, she appears to grow from "childhood ignorance to more adult knowledge," a movement expected in bildungsromane (Moji, 2015: 187). Additionally, by addressing the social and economic failures of the postcolonial state, *We Need New Names* does appear, in some ways, to share characteristics with other African novels of disillusionment. Echoing the language of waithood, disillusionment produces an "in-between state," and "a permanent state of limbo," which certainly captures the narrative world of *We Need New Names* (Moji, 2015: 185). Throughout the scenes set in Paradise, Bulawayo emphasizes the waiting that dominates the lived experience of Darling, her family, and friends.

Importantly, the transition from Zimbabwe to the United States underscores the idea that "waiting" is a shared experience rather than a point of contrast between the two countries, accentuated in the final extradiegetic chapter, "How They Lived." Sincere yet broken promises from children in America to their parents in Zimbabwe to "just wait" result in parents who "waited and they saw, saw that we did not come. They died waiting, clutching in their dried hands pictures of us leaning against the Lady Liberty" (Bulawayo, 2013: 250). The chapter concludes with the caveat that estrangement from home will mean that "the spirits will not come running to meet us, and so we will wait and wait and wait—forever waiting in the air like flags of unsung countries" (Bulawayo, 2013: 252). The temporal constraints of waithood require new social connections and strategies, and new ways of being to negotiate the temporality of pervasive waiting.

Although Bulawayo does not directly characterize Darling as fully embracing her waithood, she strongly hints at her future possibilities and defiance in one of the novel's final scenes. While studying for a biology test in her bedroom, Darling uses a marker to write "*iBio iyirabishi*" on her wall in protest (Bulawayo, 2013: 276). Unable to erase the marks, she searches for items to cover them up. In a box labeled "HOMELAND DECORATIONS," she finds several items: a batik painting of a market scene, a "copper clock in the shape of the map of our country" that is broken and "stuck at six o'clock," and a "weird mask . . . split in the center, one half white, the other black" (Bulawayo, 2013: 285). The black half is divided "further in numerous crazy patterns that I can't figure out" (Bulawayo, 2013: 285). All three items reflect the difficult present of Zimbabwe, but especially the clock—literally frozen in time like the "dead watches" of the parents who wait to vote earlier in the novel (Bulawayo, 2013: 61). What the mask signifies to Darling here is not clarified, although it might evoke the different ethnic groups of Zimbabwe, or Darling's fractured, hybrid sense of self and identity. This latter suggestion is supported by Darling's observation that the mask is "trying to tell me something that will take years for me to understand" (Bulawayo, 2013: 285), since the text does not depict Darling's development beyond this moment, nor the ways she navigates the pulls between Zimbabwe and America. After a Skype conversation with Chipo, who asserts that Zimbabwe is no longer Darling's country because she has left it, Darling throws her computer at all three objects, breaking the mask and computer. Although not able to make sense of the "weird" mask, now irreparably broken, Darling does in the end take aim at the broken clock, a manifestation of waithood and suspension.

In sum, while the incorporation and self-fulfillment characteristic of the classic bildungsroman is absent in this scene, the novel's ending does nevertheless gesture toward Darling entering a new stage. It may not be the adulthood or the consolidation of a harmonious self that the European bildungsroman displays, but *We Need New Names* exhibits characteristics of other postcolonial bildungsromane through the depiction of the temporality of waiting and waithood. These resemblances suggest that *We Need New Names* might be situated most productively in the context of not only other African bildungsromane, such as *Nervous Conditions*, but also postcolonial bildungsromane more generally. Waithood captures Darling's temporal and social experiences as a diasporic figure, but waithood itself is not the primary adversary Darling faces. On the contrary, waithood is a condition Darling inhabits and makes use of as she adjusts to the manifold pulls of belonging, difference, and desire. Like texts in other bildungsroman traditions—the feminist, the postcolonial, the African, and the African American traditions described above—*We Need New Names* narrates Darling's coming-of-age in ways that oppose and critique the structural inequalities of her specific time and place. But the temporal dimensions of waithood, coupled with a focus on Darling's prolonged girlhood, widen the frame of critique beyond Darling's local contexts to encompass global experiences of uneven development and mobility.

REFERENCES

Arnett, James. 2016. "Taking Pictures: The Economy of Affect and Postcolonial Performativity in NoViolet Bulawayo's We Need New Names." *Ariel: A Review of International English Literature* 47(3): 149–173.

Austen, Ralph A. 2015. "Struggling with the African Bildungsroman." *Research in African Literatures* 46(3): 214–231.
Boes, Tobias. 2012. *Formative Fictions: Nationalism, Cosmopolitanism, and the Bildungsroman*. Ithaca: Cornell University Press.
Bulawayo, NoViolet. 2013. *We Need New Names: A Novel*. First edition. New York: Reagan Arthur Books, Little, Brown and Company.
Dangarembga, Tsitsi. 2004. *Nervous Conditions: A Novel*. Banbury: Ayebia Clarke.
Esty, Joshua. 2012. *Unseasonable Youth: Modernism, Colonialism, and the Fiction of Development*. Modernist Literature & Culture. New York: Oxford University Press.
Felski, Rita. 1989. *Beyond Feminist Aesthetics: Feminist Literature and Social Change*. Cambridge, MA: Harvard University Press.
Goyal, Yogita. 2017. "We Need New Diasporas." *American Literary History* 29(4): 640–663.
Haas, Bridget M. 2017. "Citizens-in-Waiting, Deportees-in-Waiting: Power, Temporality, and Suffering in the U.S. Asylum System." *ETHOS* 45(1): 75–97.
Hay, Simon. 2013. "Nervous Conditions, Lukacs, and the Postcolonial Bildungsroman." *Genre* 46(3): 317–344.
Honwana, Alcinda Manuel. 2012. *The Time of Youth: Work, Social Change, and Politics in Africa*. First edition. Sterling, VA: Kumarian Press Pub.
Isaacs, Camille. 2016. "Mediating Women's Globalized Existence Through Social Media in the Work of Adichie and Bulawayo." *Safundi: The Journal of South African and American Studies* 17(2): 174–188.
Jeffrey, Craig. 2010. *Timepass: Youth, Class, and the Politics of Waiting in India*. Stanford, CA: Stanford University Press.
Kester, Gunilla Theander. 1995. *Writing the Subject: Bildung and the African American Text*. American University Studies, vol. 54. New York: P. Lang.
Masquelier, Adeline. 2013. "Teatime: Boredom and the Temporalities of Young Men in Niger." *Africa: The Journal of the International African Institute* 83(3): 385–402.
Moji, Polo Belina. 2015. "New Names, Translational Subjectivities: (Dis)Location and (Re)Naming in NoViolet Bulawayo's We Need New Names." *Journal of African Cultural Studies* 27(2): 181–190.
Moretti, Franco. 1987. *The Way of the World: The Bildungsroman in European Culture*. London: Verso.
Muponde, Robert. 2015. *Some Kinds of Childhood: Images of History and Resistance in Zimbabwean Literature*. Trenton: Africa World Press.
Ndlovu, Isaac. 2016. "Ambivalence of Representation: African Crises, Migration and Citizenship in NoViolet Bulawayo's We Need New Names." *African Identities* 14(2): 132–146.
Nyatetũ-Waigwa, Wangari wa. 1996. *The Liminal Novel: Studies in the Francophone-African Novel as Bildungsroman*. American University Studies, vol. 6. New York: Peter Lang.
Quayson, Ato. 2014. *Oxford Street, Accra: City Life and the Itineraries of Transnationalism*. Durham: Duke University Press.
Slaughter, Joseph R. 2007. *Human Rights, Inc.: The World Novel, Narrative Form, and International Law*. New York: Fordham University Press.

Sommers, Marc. 2012. *Stuck: Rwandan Youth and the Struggle for Adulthood*. Studies in Security and International Affairs. Athens, GA: [Washington, D.C.]: University of Georgia Press; published in association with the United States Institute of Peace.

Tibaijuka, Anna Kajumulo. 2005. "Report of the Fact-Finding Mission to Zimbabwe to Assess the Scope and Impact of Operation Murambatsvina." *United Nations Special Envoy on Human Settlements Issues in Zimbabwe*. http://www.un.org/News/dh/infocus/zimbabwe/zimbabwe_rpt.pdf.

Chapter 4

Sexuality, Resilience, and Mobility in Amma Darko's *Beyond the Horizon* and Chika Unigwe's *On Black Sisters' Street*

Tomi Adeaga

The transatlantic slave trade subjected both male and female Africans to forced migration across the Atlantic Ocean to the Americas, Europe, and to other parts of the world. In the global age however, the exploitation and denigration of young African women through transatlantic prostitution networks culminate in what may be called modern-day forced slavery/migrations. While the transatlantic slave trade exposed African women to rape and sexual exploitation by their slave owners, this new form of bondage ensures the commodification of African women in the global age. Against this background, this chapter examines prostitution as modern-day slavery in the form of sex work in the novels of two contemporary female African authors, Amma Darko in *Beyond the Horizon* (1988) and Chika Unigwe in *On Black Sisters Street* (2009). Special focus will also be given to magical realism as a form of cultural agency in *On Black Sisters' Street*. The chapter explores the question of whether the sex work by the women in the two novels that are located in Germany and Belgium can be called forced modern-day slavery or sex-trafficking. The chapter also highlights the dynamics of sisterhood, in *On Black Sisters' Street* along with magical realism that is rooted in African traditional cultures.

   Globalization has encouraged movements across the world and through the influence of social developments in various regions of Africa, transatlantic migration has become a source of income and survival for many Africans. These movements have also exposed migrants to human-trafficking and females are especially vulnerable. While the debate over contemporary human-trafficking dates back to the nineteenth century in Great Britain, it was intensified in the twentieth century through different international agreements and conventions. Article 3 of the UNTC defines human trafficking as:

> "Trafficking in persons" shall mean the recruitment, transportation, transfer, harbouring or receipt of persons, by means of the threat or use of force or other forms of coercion, of abduction, of fraud, of deception, of the abuse of power or of a position of vulnerability or of the giving or receiving of payments or benefits to achieve the consent of a person having control over another person, for the purpose of exploitation. Exploitation shall include at a minimum, the exploitation of the prostitution of others or other forms of sexual exploitation, forced labour or services, slavery or practices similar to slavery, servitude or the removal of organs. (2)

Human traffickers, aware of the risks involved in the trafficking of human beings, have created sophisticated channels and networks for the easy and undetected flow of trafficked persons from Africa into Europe.

Against this background, this chapter explores the dynamics of how the characters confront the challenges posed to them by prostitution in Germany and Belgium. Addressing this issue of prostitution and global sex trafficking, Holly Wardlow contends that "there has been heated debate . . . about how prostitution should be understood . . . there has been some basic agreement that of the various terms to choose from, *sex work*, in particular, is a better label—better in that it may more accurately represent what women feel they are doing when they engage in monetized sexual exchanges (i.e., working) and their reasons for doing so (i.e., economic need)" (Wardlow, 2004: 1017).

The ongoing debate invokes the use of the term "sex workers" as opposed to prostitution because of its relevance to the works examined. This is especially important since prostitution suggests willingness to engage in sex work for reasons other than financial gain. However, sex-trafficking is purely about financial gains, that is selling one's body or that of others for money. This is, in essence what all the women in the novels are doing.

SEXUALITY AND RESILIENCY IN AMMA DARKO'S *BEYOND THE HORIZON*

Amma Darko's first novel, *Beyond the Horizon* narrates the life of the protagonist, Mara Ajaman. In this novel, Mara's journey begins in her village of Naka, moves to the city after her marriage to Akobi Ajaman (Cobby), and ends in a brothel in Germany. At the beginning of the narrative, Mara is presented as an innocent girl overwhelmed by the fact that of all the beautiful women in her village, she is singled out by Akobi. His family is rich and he could have married a girl from an equally wealthy family but instead, he chose her. Mara's expectations of marriage conform to norms of domesticated life and submissive behavior toward her husband, irrespective of how he behaves toward her. And indeed, he treats her badly. Mara's marriage to Akobi is described as one in which she is exploited from the beginning of their relationship. The most glaring exploitation takes place when he comes to the village to see his wife and newborn son, Kofo. Akobi's father categorically refuses to "give in to his demand that he should sell part of his farmlands and give him the money for some projects he was about to undertake which would, guaranteed, bring in plenty of money" (Darko, 1988: 30). Unable to tap into his father's resources, he sells her belongings to buy his ticket to Germany. In search of her prized treasures, Mara laments that "I looked and found nothing; neither the jewelry nor my new clothes. And the costly waistbeads I inherited from my grandmother when she died I didn't find. Plus other little things, all of which were gone, even the little carving mother had given me the first time I was leaving for the city as my protector" (Darko, 1988: 31).

Alluding to these lies and fabrications about a continent that Akobi has never visited, Célestine Gbaguidi concurs with Edmond Cros in drawing a parallel between a literary work and the society in which it is deeply rooted. She insists that "we can point out that Amma Darko's novel under scrutiny somehow depicts situations leading some young Africans to take the decision to leave for the Promised Land, Europe. There is often a clear-cut difference between a European's lifestyle and that of an African; and willing to match the European's lifestyle, some poverty-stricken and desperate Africans make for Europe" (Gbaguidi, 2014: 40).

Ironically, despite Akobi's looting of Mara's belongings to travel to Germany, she is not discouraged about her uncertain future, and naively joins him there. She allows herself to be smuggled into Germany because she believes that she will resume her duties as his wife. In so doing, she becomes one of those women whom Liz Kelly and Linda Regan have summed up as those who are "never made aware of the extent to which they will be indebted, intimidated, exploited and controlled. They believe ... that they can travel to a richer country and earn large amounts of money in a short space of time, which they can use to move themselves and their families out of poverty and despair" (Kelly and Regan, 2000: 24).

Mara is smuggled into Germany by human-traffickers. When she arrives, she learns that Akobi already has an illegal German wife, Gitte with whom he lives. He adds insult to injury by making her live in the same apartment with Gitte to whom he introduces as his sister. She is forced to endure these indignities as she becomes essentially a house-help for them and watches them sleep in the same bed. She admits that "this coldness I feel does not grip my body so much as it does my soul. It's deep inside me that feels this chilliness, from the dejected soul my body habours, a soul grown old from too much use of its shelter. . . . I've used myself and allowed myself to be used to care any longer" (Darko, 1988: 1).

Since she is in Germany illegally, and is financially dependent on Akobi, he sells her into modern-day slavery. According to Danailova-Trainor and Laczko, "human trafficking has been described as a form of modern-day slavery, which deprives people of their human rights and freedoms" (Danailova-Trainor and Laczko, 1). Hernandez and Rudolph, maintain that "the illicit activity of Trafficking in Persons (TIP), often acknowledged as 'modern-day slavery,' bases its source of profits on the exploitation of human rights by using people as commodities" (Hernandez and Rudolph, 0). Thus, modern-day slavery goes against the Universal Declaration of Human Rights (UDHR) in which Article 3 plainly states that "Everyone has the right to life, liberty and security of person." But, these are precisely the rights that are taken from Mara as she is blackmailed and sold by Akobi and his friend Osey. She is handed over to Pompey, the owner of a brothel called *Peepy*. In order to accomplish this, Akobi and his friend, Osey, first of all make Mara watch a pornographic film and her reaction to it is revealing. She thinks to herself:

> This action film that I saw horrified me and left me sitting in my seat heated up with my mouth open. The people on the screen, they were . . . that is to say, they were several men and women all together; about fifteen or so; among them, black women, Africans; and they were doing it there . . . there on the screen! They were actually doing the thing plain plain there on the screen before everybody. And there was no trace of shame or whatever on their faces. Not one bit! It was a shock for me, my first shock, my first horror. (Darko, 1988: 68)

Mara's expression of horror over the explicit sex is indeed her first, intense shock. Ironically, "at this point in Darko's story, Mara is still ignorant of the fact that she is going to go through a similar sexual ritual of initiation" (Frías, 2000: 8). Indeed, Mara displays the innocence of a woman who has never been exposed to sexually explicit acts, and who also does not envisage herself being in a similar situation where she is intimate with men other than Akobi. But the scales fall from her eyes as Akobi and Osey show her a video they secretly made of her having sex with several men after she is drugged and unable to resist. They threaten to send the video to her family back home. Mara, a mother of two sons is told by Akobi that, "Mara Mara, oh Mara, even if you don't want to, you will still have to. For, an illegal nigger woman like you, there is no other job in Germany. Mara, if you don't get a housemaid job then there's only this. You understand? Because you are too illegal and too black for any proper job, you get it?" (Darko, 1988: 114). Here, Akobi takes advantage of Mara's ignorance of the German laws that protect women in her situation, and tells her that she is not worth more than a house help or a prostitute. By emphasizing her illegal status, he unequivocally bonds her in servitude. He makes it clear that the sole purpose for smuggling her into Germany is to sell her for a price. His plan is to use this money to finance his lavish lifestyle with other women. Unknown to Mara, he had taken Comfort, his girlfriend and former colleague in the Ministries, to live in Germany before he sent for her. Akobi dehumanizes his legal wife and turns her into a slave in Germany. The length of time that it takes her to realize this begs for an understanding of the author's rationale for projecting her as a woman unable to rise above her difficulties.

Mara's voice is silenced by Akobi's oppressive treatment toward her and she does not fight back immediately. Instead, Darko allows her to experience a litany of suffering, and indignities in her marriage. Mara's humiliation and suffering that dominate most of the narrative are like drawing a long, deep breath before she finally decides to resist. She wakes from her deep inertia to fight against the ignominies that Akobi has subjected her to throughout their marriage.

But this newly found willingness to change her destiny is unable to alter her fate. Udechukwu Peter Umezurike contends in this regard that "Mara's realisation to resist ideology is animated by her recognition of her loss of dignity. She realises that she is left with nothing, having lost virtually every form of meaning in her life, her relationship with her family, mother and her two children. Worse still, Akobi the husband whom she has tried so much to please and serve has robbed her of this dignity" (Umezurike, 2015: 157). Once Mara regains control of herself, she plots her escape from Akobi with the help of Kaye, a fellow African woman and wife of Pompey, the owner of *Peepy*, the brothel where she works. Kaye readily agrees as she explicitly rejoins that "at last, Mara! You have woken up. I have been waiting for you to wake up by yourself. I could have woken you up, of course, but in this business, which operates in a world of its own and is far colder than the cold world outside, it is always better to wake up by yourself. Only then do you fight to remain awake because you know how difficult that waking up has been and what a long time and a lot of thinking it takes. And you also know what it means to be asleep" (Darko, 1988: 119). Mara's agency to shape the trajectory of her life displays her resilience in the face of her suffering. But Mara's resiliency only comes to the fore as it is too late to make much difference. Even after settling scores with Akobi and Osey, by having Akobi thrown in prison for fraud among other things, she comes to the realization that her experience as a prostitute has left indelible emotional trauma. The drugs that she used while working at *Peepy* affected her so deeply that she was too ashamed to return home to Ghana. Her life as a prostitute and drug addict in Germany would bring shame to her children and family.

SEXUALITY AND MOBILITY IN CHIKA UNIGWE'S *ON BLACK SISTERS' STREET*

With reference to discursive engagement with appropriate terminology describing international sex work, Michelle O.P. Dunbar states that, "the question of whether trafficking in women should be considered under the slavery ideology is an ongoing debate in the international arena. While trafficking in women may not meet all the criteria of the traditional definition of "slavery," the practices of sex trafficking, and forced labor do share similar elements that deem them obvious candidates for inclusion under "modern forms of slavery" (Dunbar, 1999: 115). Furthermore, human-trafficking as a literary theme has increased over the past 20 years, especially as young girls and women continue to be trafficked for money either voluntarily or involuntarily. The fundamental elements of trafficking in women is underscored by Dunbar and include:

> The abusive or servile situation the women are in and whether there is consent. Physical travel or transport is necessary under most definitions of trafficking in women. Trafficking may have the same effect on the victim if they are moved 5 miles across a state border or 500 miles within national boundaries.... Thus, a key issue that surrounds the trafficking element is that the victims are moved to different and perhaps unfamiliar surroundings. These victims are isolated and most often held in areas where they may not even understand the language. They have no legal identity as a result of confiscated documents, and they are at the mercy of their traffickers for subsistence. (Dunbar, 1999: 105–106)

Chika Unigwe's *On Black Sisters' Street* (2009) highlights the unfortunate plight of most of the young girls and women ensnared by human-trafficking across the world. Unigwe is a storyteller who explores the issue of forced migration through transnational human-trafficking. This novel is compelling because even though it is a work of fiction, it conveys a realistic portrait of the fate of many migrant African women who are sex workers in brothels across Europe, and other sites in the West. *On Black Sisters' Street*, narrates a vivid account that resonates with Akachi Adimora Ezeigbo's *Trafficked* (2008). Similar to Ezeigbo, Unigwe includes authentic locations in Nigeria to illustrate the circumstances that lead the women into the sex trade. *Trafficked* portrays the young protagonist, Nneoma who leaves her fiancé Ofomata and is smuggled to Italy by human-traffickers. She escapes and is subsequently deported to Lagos, Nigeria.

Unigwe taps into the history of Nigerian collective feminist activism in the sense that the women characters are only able to overcome their problems when they join forces. In this instance, Unigwe incorporates the collective voices of the four women, Ama, Efe, Joyce, and Sisi in a brothel on Zwartezusterstraat in Antwerp, Belgium, represented by the main narrator, Sisi, a voice from the dead. What these four women have in common is their being trafficked as sex workers by a Nigerian businessman called Dele Senghor. Chielozona Eze observes that "Dele's use of the phrase 'passage to Europe' is one of Unigwe's deliberate acts of association with transatlantic slavery, the Middle Passage. In so doing, she provides readers with answers to the question of what these displaced bodies in pain reveal about human rights in Africa" (Darko, 1988: 92). The phrase, "passage to Europe" not only links contemporary, forced immigration to the transatlantic slave trade but it also interrogates the historical significance to the vulnerability of African subjects to exploitation. This passage to Europe is "forced migration" because the social, economic, and political factors that drive women into such unholy alliances with their smugglers are often rooted in different socio-political dysfunctions at work in the women's home countries.

In Nigeria, illiteracy due to poverty, chronic unemployment among university graduates, as well as family commitments, are some of the root causes. Unemployment and subsequent poverty forces graduates to search for other means of survival. Some migrate to other parts of Africa and to Western nations. Many people embark on the perilous journey to cross the Atlantic Ocean in search of economic opportunities. Females that are less fortunate may end up in brothels where they are robbed of their freedom as their passports are taken away, leaving them at the mercy of those who arranged their travel.

In Sudan, civil war between the northern and southern parts of the region is a major factor that has driven some of the inhabitants to other parts of the continent and beyond. Also, many of them end up in refugee camps from where they are either taken or smuggled to Europe. They migrate with the hope of escaping the misery of ethnic conflict but end up in another form of slavery. This in essence is the central theme in Unigwe's narration. The four women in her novel come from different nations, socioeconomic backgrounds, and experiences. Ama grew up in a middle-class Christian family in Enugu, Nigeria. Ama's father, a pastor whom everybody in his church called Brother Cyril wore white safari suits as a sign of his holiness. But he starts raping his daughter from the age of eight. When she confronts him and says to her mother, "do you know what he did to me when I was little? He raped me. Night after night, he would come to my room and force me to spread my legs for him (Unigwe, 2009: 147). Ama's mother does not believe her and takes sides with her father. Her mother sends her away the next day to Lagos to live with her mother's cousin, Mama *Eko*. She works in Mama *Eko's buka* or local eatery for some months, until Dele Senghor, one of her customers offers to send her abroad where she would earn more money.

Another of the women is Efe, whose mother is dead and her father drowns his sorrow in alcohol. She shares a small flat with him and her three siblings in Lagos, Nigeria. She has an affair with the 45-year-old Titus, a married man who leaves her once she gets pregnant. She starts working in Dele's office until he offers her a job abroad as a sex-worker in the house in Zwartezusterstraat in Antwerp, Belgium. Sisi is also a Nigerian woman who makes the decision to work in a foreign country after remaining unemployed for more than two years. Her only prospect for stability is marrying her boyfriend Peter and living on his meager salary.

Similarly, Joyce, whose birth name is Alek, travels from Sudan to Antwerp. She is caught in the Sudanese civil war during which the members of her family were killed by the *Janjaweed* militia. Like many civil war survivors, she is raped before she is rescued by the United Nations peace workers and taken to a refugee camp. In this camp, she meets and falls in love with one of the workers, Polycarp, an Igbo soldier from Nigeria who takes her back to Lagos, with the intention of marrying her. After his mother rejects the marriage because she is not an Igbo woman, Polycarp gets rid of her by paying for her passage to Antwerp.

The women are from different social, ethnic, and cultural backgrounds, and they are all forced into sex work by circumstances often beyond their control. These socioeconomic and political circumstances of their lives drive them into the hands of Dele Senghor (Dele), who lives in Lagos, Nigeria, and his enabler, Madam Kate in the brothel house on Zwartezusterstraat, Antwerp in Belgium. Dele's business is called: "Dele and Sons Ltd: Import-Export Specialists" (Unigwe, 2009: 78). Ironically, the sex industry that Dele runs appears so simple at first glance. All the girls have to do is to remain naïve and vulnerable while he provides the passage and the fake passports that will admit them into the countries' ports of entry. He charges them 30,000 Euros each, which they will pay him once they have settled into the sex work. Once they get to the brothel house on Zwartezusterstraat, their passports are seized by Madam Kate. She sends them to the Ministry of Foreign Affairs where they are forced to notify the authorities of the loss of their passports. As a result, they are forced to become indentured servants to Dele. Eze concludes that "Dele is a synecdoche for the patriarchs of his society; his relation to women is that of master to his servants. Women exist in his life to serve his material needs, which includes functioning as sex slaves" (Eze, 2016: 147). The women are disposable, replaceable commodities that represent the financial values that he has placed on their heads, and they are treated as such.

At the end of the day, Sisi's attempt to escape is forever halted by Kate's handyman, Segun. He is the fixer who oversees everything in the brothel, including ending the women's lives if they try to escape their bondage. While they are in his car, he hits her with a hammer and kills her. Dele tries to justify the murder to Kate on the phone, that "Yes. Yes, Kate. I trust you. I trust you to take the necessary steps. Dat gal just fin' my trouble. She cost me money. How much money you pay the police? . . . Tell de gals make them no try insubordinate me. I warn all da gals, nobody dey mess with Senghor Dele. Nobody! You treat these gals well and wetin dey go do? Just begin misbehave. Imagine! . . . Na good worker we lose but gals *boku* for Lagos" (Unigwe, 2009: 295). Here, Dele admits that he ordered the killing of Sisi. She is just one of the many girls he sends into sexual slavery and her death is a mere loss of money which will be recuperated. After all as he says above, "gals *boku*" for Lagos, which means that there are many girls waiting in line to replace her.

Fluid mobility and spatiotemporality arehighlighted through Sisi's wandering around the city of Antwerp, which Daria Tunca observes is "a habit she already developed in Lagos, also seems to testify to her wish to escape her own existence" (Tunca, 2009: 12). While Tunca is accurate in her assessments, the broad picture lies in the Igbo/African cultural traditions that link such wanderings to magical realism. Here, Sisi wanders across the city of Antwerp while she is alive and journeys across the Atlantic Ocean to Nigeria at death. Both wanderings that transcend life and death are elements of the Abiku/Ogbanje children among the Yoruba and Igbo of Nigeria that travel frequently between life and death. According to Timothy Mobolade, "an Abiku is any child who dies and is reborn several times into the same family; hence, the life-span of an Abiku is characteristically very short indeed" (Mobolade, 1973: 62). Sisi's continued wanderings after death corroborate the belief that the Abiku/Ogbanje phenomenon transcends the afterlife in search of a new womb to enter.

According to Christopher N. Okonkwo, "'ogbanje' and 'abiku' are Igbo and Yoruba names, respectively, for a spirit-child or spirit-children who are said to die early only to be reborn again and again to the same mother. The belief/idea is so gripping, enduring, and widespread that researchers have noted its existence proper and/or its variants among other Nigerian, West African, and Diasporic African communities"(Okonkwo, 2004: 653). As Douglas McCabe demonstrates in his introduction to "Born-to-Die"—a recent study that explores the historicity and politics of Ogbanje and Abiku in Nigerian letters: "the authochthonicity and socio-literary imaginings of the belief have not remained impermeable to socio-historical, geopolitical, cultural, or discursive and literary practices and exchanges" (Okonkwo, 2004: 653). Douglas McCabe also adds that "*Abiku* literally means 'one who is born, dies'—though the compact 'born to die,' with its implication of a fated or deliberately planned death, has become the standard translation. *Ifá babaláwo* apply the term to children who have secret plans to die at a certain time in their upbringing, only to be born again soon afterwards, repeating this itinerary of death and birth until they are spiritually 'fettered' (de) by their parents and forced to stay in the world" (McCabe, 2002: 46).

Unigwe's usage of this narrative element is also a means of accentuating the displacement of these women through this middle passage. However, historically, magical realism in Nigerian literature dates back to works by D.O. Fagunwa, in his *Ògbójú Ọdẹ nínú Igbó Irúnmalẹ̀* (1938) (English title: *The Forest of a Thousand Daemons,* 1968), Amos Tutuola's *The Palm-Wine Drinkard* (1954), and Chinua Achebe's *Things Fall Apart* (1958). The palm-wine drinkard in Tutuola's narration travels from the land of the living to the land of the dead in search of his dead palm-wine tapster. In the process, he has to overcome many hindrances placed in his way by different magical creatures. In the same vein, Achebe makes use of the *Ogbanje* phenomenon as an agent of magical realism in *Things Fall Apart*. In this novel, the author portrays Okonkwo's favorite daughter Ezinma, who falls ills all the time and is identified as an *ogbanje* child. Chikwenye Okonjo Ogunyemi asserts that this *ogbanje* child becomes a:

> Frequent traveler between the world of the living and the place of the friendly dead. From here, her play-mates incessantly beckon for reunion; that is, a separation from parents and home. (The Igbo verb je is "to go," while nje means "come on," indicating urgency and the need for a response.) Ogbanje predicates a metaphysical and political discomfort with life, aggravated by the instability of coming from the otherworld to frequent this world. Ogbanje is constantly on the move, and her presence highlights the insecurities of an exiled/nomadic status. The tenacity of the precocious ogbanje as child magician and tactician and as an idea moves the diagnosis of the disorder beyond individual pathology. (Ogunyemi, 2002: 664)

Like an *ogbanje* child, who travels between three worlds, the terrestrial, the spiritual, and the bush, Sisi travels frequently between three worlds, the spiritual world, Europe, and Africa. The spatiotemporal dimensions ensure fluidity in the novel as the reader embarks on the journey of re-remembering through flashbacks, the situation that leads to Sisi's untimely death through her own eyes, and in her own voice after death.

Through her "spiritual" voice, Sisi also exposes Kate as a tool of exploitation of her fellow African sisters by highlighting her role in her life and death at the brothel. As the *madam*, Kate takes on patriarchal qualities as she aligns herself with Dele to exploit the four women. Sisi's death has an outcome that both Kate and Dele did not anticipate in that it transforms and galvanizes Joyce, Ama, and Efe into action. At death, Sisi becomes an inspiration for Ama, Efe, and Joyce, who hardly took the time to get to know each other while she was alive. Sisi's death becomes the rallying cry for sisterhood, that comes as Efe suddenly "adjusts her wig, pulling it down so that the fringe almost covers her eyebrows. Her eyes are far away, fixed at a memory that starts to rise and again shape in front of her: 'I used to know a man who sold good-quality weave-on'" (Unigwe, 2009: 40). With this sentence, Efe sets the stage for something greater, that will bind them all together for life. Ama and Joyce are surprised at Efe's words to them. It is the first time that Efe has spoken about her life before she came to Antwerp. These women who have been thrown together and forced to live and work in the same brothel bond together after Sisi's death. The sudden realization that Sisi is dead is an initiation to sisterhood.

CONCLUSION

On Black Sisters Street and *Beyond the Horizon* are authored by African female writers who examine sex-trafficking and modern-day slavery. The women in both works have been forced into sex-trafficking, often by poverty, and situations beyond their control. But what sets the two texts apart and which is also representative of contemporary African authors is their modern approach to feminism that is also result oriented in the sense that when faced with various challenges the female characters find solutions to their problems. These include breaking away from male dominance, often aided by other female associates. In Unigwe's novel, before leaving their countries, Nigeria and Sudan, most of the women are unaware of what awaits them in Belgium because they have never engaged in sex work. Even those who do know or have an inkling of their fate are shocked by the circumstances under which they are forced to work. Neither does Darko's main character, Mara, know the kind of life she will be forced to live when she is smuggled to Germany. While the characters in both novels negotiate their oppression differently, the impact of prostitution as a means of survival for the characters in the two novels still remains the same.

The women in the two novels convey the message that this line of work is not their first choice and under other circumstances, they would have chosen something different. In *On Black Sisters' Street*, after paying off their debt to Dele, Ama and Joyce go back to Nigeria where Ama opens a boutique and Joyce establishes a primary and a secondary school. It is only Efe, who chooses to remain in Belgium and set up a brothel. In *Beyond the Horizon*, after having taken her revenge on Akobi and Osey, Mara keeps on working in Pompey's brothel, *Peepy*.

One of the other questions posed at the beginning of this chapter is whether human-trafficking in Germany and Belgium in the two novels should be called modern-day slavery or voluntary work. The answer is that it is indeed a form of modern-day slavery because of the invisible walls of restrictions that the European nations erect. These barriers are requirements for self-identification and legal status in the form of passports and identity cards. Without these forms of identification, the person does not exist. The lack of documentation is common to all the trafficked women in Unigwe's and Darko's novels. Moreover, Sisi loses her life while trying to reclaim her identity as Chisom. Given that unlike Sisi who in her lifetime is unable to exert her revenge on Dele and Kate, Darko ensures that Mara does take her revenge on Akobi by sending him to prison in Germany. Finally, both novels display the ways in which the effects of sex-trafficking in the global era is the immediate loss of agency among African women. In order to survive, they are forced to engage in sex work. If they do not comply, they feel the pains of their slave-masters' whip, which can even lead to their deaths, the way Sisi's life is prematurely brought to an end.

REFERENCES

Achebe, Chinua. 1958. *Things Fall Apart*. London: Heinemann.
Adimora-Ezeigbo, Akachi. 2008. *Trafficked*. Lagos: Lantern Books.
Danailova-Trainor, Gergana, and Frank Laczko. 2010. "Trafficking in Persons and Development: Towards Greater Policy Coherence." *International Migration*, edited by Elizbieta Gozdziak July 19, 2010. doi:10.1111/j.1468-2435.2010.00625.x
Darko, Amma. 1989. *Beyond the Horizon*. Great Britain: Heinemann.
Dunbar, Michelle O. P. 1999. "The Past, Present, and Future of International Trafficking in Women for Prostitution." *Buffalo Women's Law Journal*, Vol. 8, Article 17: 103–128. https://digitalcommons.law.buffalo.edu/bwlj/vol8/iss1/17
Eze, Chielozona. 2014."Feminism with a Big "F": Ethics and the Rebirth of African Feminism in Chika Unigwe's On Black Sisters' Street." *Research in African Literatures*, Vol. 45, No. 4 (Winter): 89–103.
Eze, Chielozona. 2016. "The Enslaved Body as Symbol of Universal Human Rights Abuse: Chika Unigwe." *Ethics and Human Rights in Anglophone African Women's Literature: Feminist Empathy*, 145–163. USA: Palgrave Macmillan.
Fagunwa, D. O. 1939. *Forest of a Thousand Daemons (A Hunter's Tale)*. Translated by Wole Soyinka. San Francisco: City of Lights.
Frías, María. 2000. "Women on Top: Prostitution and Pornography in Amma Darko's Beyond the Horizon." *Wasafiri*, Vol. 17, No. 37: 8–13. doi:10.1080/02690050208589799
Gbaguidi, Célestine. 2014. "African Illegal Immigrants' Disillusionment in Europe: A Study of Amma Darko's." *Beyond the Horizon: REVUE DU CAMES 'Littératures, Langues et linguistique' Semestriel de publication du CAMES*, Vol. 2, No. 2: 37–48. http://publication.lecames.org/index.php/lit/article/view/303
Hernandez, Diego, and Alexandra Rudolph. 2011. "Modern Day Slavery: What Drives Human Trafficking in Europe?" *Courant Research Centre: Poverty, Equity*

and Growth: Discussion Papers, No. 97, Courant Research Centre Poverty, Equity and Growth, (Göttingen, 2011). https://www.econstor.eu/bitstream/10419/90504/1/CRC-PEG_DP_97.pdf

Kelly, Liz, and Linda Regan. 2002. *Stopping Traffic: Exploring the Extent of, and Responses to Trafficking in Women for Sexual Exploitation in the UK*, Vol. 36. Home Office, Policing and Reducing Crime Unit.

McCabe, Douglas. 2002. "Histories of Errancy: Oral Yoruba "Àbíkú" Texts and Soyinka's "Abiku." *Research in African Literatures*, Vol. 33, No. 1 (Spring): 45–74. https://www.jstor.org/stable/3820929

Mobolade, Timothy. 1973. "The Concept of Abiku." *African Arts*, Vol. 7, No. 1 (Autumn): 62–64. http://www.jstor.org/stable/3334754

Ogunyemi, Chikwenye Okonjo. 2002. "An Abiku-Ogbanje Atlas: A Pre-Text for Rereading Soyinka's "Aké" and Morrison's "Beloved." *African American Review*, Vol. 36, No. 4 (Winter): 663–678. http://www.jstor.org/stable/1512424

Okonkwo, Christopher N. 2004. "A Critical Divination: Reading Sula as Ogbanje-Abiku." *African American Review*, Vol. 38, No. 4 (Winter): 651–668. http://www.jstor.com/stable/4134423

Rosen, Liana W. 2017. "Human Trafficking: New Global Estimates of Forced Labor and Modern Slavery." *CRS Insight*. October 18, 2017 (IN10803): n.pag. https://www.hsdl.org/?view&did=805242

Tunca, Daria. 2009. "Redressing the "Narrative Balance": Subjection and Subjectivity in Chika Unigwe's Black Sisters' Street." *Journal of Afroeuropean Studies, Afroeuropa* 31: n.pag.

Tutola, Amos. 1954. *The Palm Wine Drinkard.* London: Heinemann.

Umezurike, Uchechukwu Peter. 2015. "Resistance in Amma Darko's Beyond the Horizon and Chika Unigwe's On Black Sisters' Street." *An International Journal of Language, Literature and Gender Studies (LALIGENS), Ethiopia*, Vol. 4, No. 2, Serial No. 10 (May): 152–163. http://dx.doi.org/10.4314/laligens.v4i2.11

Unigwe, Chika. 2009. *On Black Sisters Street.* London: Jonathan Cape.

United Nations. 2018. "The Universal Declaration of Human Rights." Accessed October 30, 2018. http://www.un.org/en/universal-declaration-human-rights/

Wardlow, Holly. 2004. "Anger, Economy, and Female Agency: Problematizing "Prostitution" and "Sex Work" Among the Huli of Papua New Guinea." *Signs*, Vol. 29, No. 4 (Summer): 1017–1040. http://www.jstor.org/stable/10.1086/382628

"1933 International Convention for the Suppression of the Traffic in Women of Full Age." Accessed August 12, 2019. https://ec.europa.eu/anti-trafficking/sites/antitrafficking/files/1933_international_convention_en_1.pdf

Chapter 5

Transnational African Women as Voices of Conscience

Aidoo's Our Sister Killjoy, Adichie's Americanah, *and* Atta's A Bit of Difference

Nancy Henaku

This chapter analyzes representations of three African fictional characters—Sissie (in Aidoo's *Our Sister Killjoy,*1977), Ifemelu (in Adichie's *Americanah,* 2013), and Deola (in Atta's *A Bit Difference,* 2013/2015)—to illustrate the ways in which transnational feminist perspectives frame contemporary African women's writing and provide an oppositional aesthetic that interrogates dominant representations of black female subjects as powerless figures. Foregrounding the connections between mobility, gazing, and speaking, the chapter argues that these characters' movements across (and negotiation of identities in) varied borders and spaces allow them (and the reader) to clearly *see* complex manifestations of oppression and are subsequently able to *speak* truth to power. Through their "oppositional consciousness" (Sandoval, 1991: 10–17) as female and "Third World" subjects, transnational African fictional characters, like Sissie, Deola, and Ifemelu can become—in Spivak's (1994/1985) words—"pious item[s]" (104) providing a counter-rhetoric to global inequalities and injustices. That is, these characters, because of their unique transnational positionality, become voices of conscience speaking back and across borders. The chapter begins by discussing extant critiques of cultural misrepresentations of African female subjectivity, followed by an examination of the transnational elements of *Our Sister Killjoy, Americanah,* and *A Bit Difference,* and finally, an analysis of the political import of this transnational aesthetics.

THEORIZING CULTURAL MISREPRESENTATIONS OF AFRICAN WOMEN

Underlying this chapter's argument is an engagement with Spivak's (1994/1985) oft-cited question, "Can the subaltern (as woman) speak?" (92) and her thesis, "The subaltern as female cannot be heard or read" (104). While Spivak's point seems pessimistic, it nonetheless interrogates the liberatory possibilities of subaltern representations and in essence raises critical questions that highlight the relations between politics, ethics, and aesthetics (Cornell, 2010: 100–101). Critical perspectives on literary representations of African female subjects and hegemonic feminist discourse identify problematic tropes about non-Western women that further reinforce Spivak's argument. The link between these perspectives is taken a step further with the claim that a transnational feminist critique takes us, at least in part, out of the quandary that Spivak's reasoning raises and within such a frame of analysis, the political and rhetorical agency of transnational female literary subjects—like Sissie, Ifemelu, and Deola—become apparent.

Mohanty (2003) argues that representational homogenization in Western discourse deprives "Third World" women of "historical and political agency" (39) because, in this problematic view, they are only seen as "poor, uneducated, tradition-bound . . . victimized" (22). Clarifying the political import of these monolithic representations, Mohanty suggests that such misrepresentations construct "originary power divisions" and thus "locks all revolutionary struggles into binary structures" (38–39). In calling for an extension of our purview beyond "the Marx who found it possible to say: they cannot represent themselves; they must be represented" (42), Mohanty underscores the limitations even of the most radical thoughts in Western humanism and the role that Western feminism plays in the perpetuation of colonial ideologies about Third World subjectivities.

Mohanty's critique aligns with Busia's (1989) observations that the voiceless African female is a dominant motif in colonial writing; however, Busia, in response to Spivak, also posits that while such representations deprive African female subjects of rhetorical agency, "the systematic refusal to hear our speech is not the same as our silence. That we have hitherto been spoken of as absent or silenced does not mean we have been so" (103). Busia's argument resolves the "Kantian bias toward the active Western speaker" that Maggio (2007: 438) identifies in Spivak's argument but it raises another question: what is the essence of speaking if the subaltern cannot be heard? Read together, Spivak's (1994/1985) and Busia's (1989) arguments interrogate the politics of subaltern literary portraiture as well as the politics of reading postcolonial literature, including those written by African female authors.

These misrepresentations are not limited to colonial discourse for African male authors especially have been critiqued for portraying African women as docile, voiceless, and invisible (Newell, 2006: 138). This is obvious in the early writings, most of which were authored by men, and explore the sociopolitical impacts of colonialism (Davies, 1986: 3). Despite their rhetoric about subverting colonial representations of African subjectivity, canonical male writing often works within a problematic gendered script that produces Western philosophical binarisms: male/female, mind/body, subject/object, self/other, domination/subordination, speaker/addressee (Stratton, 1994: 41). Such misrepresentations not only sustain patriarchy but also provide a simplistic view of African women's material conditions and roles (Newell, 2006: 138). This situation is complicated by the fact that African women's literary interventions have been historically misread, if not patronized or ignored by critics (Zulfiqar, 2016: 4–7; Davies and Fido, 1993: 311–312). Thus, discussions of African women's writing require considerations of the positionality of the female writer in the African literary canon and its implication for female literary voicing. Ironically, African female authors are said to be complicit in these misrepresentations (Ogundipe-Leslie, 1994: 57–67).

For Ogundipe-Leslie, "these false images" must be revised; however, such an enterprise requires "[t]he African female writer . . . [to]be committed . . . as a writer . . . woman and . . . Third World person" (61–63). As a Third World subject, the African female author must be "politically conscious"—that is, her writing should enlighten readers on matters relating to the effects of the [neo-]colonial enterprise on Third World experiences (64). In asking African female writers to be committed as Third World people, Ogundipe-Leslie was calling for a movement beyond national and continental concerns toward a transnational view of oppression and inequality because the exploration of the African predicament in African women's writing cannot be disengaged from the forces of global imperialism and neocolonialism (65).

Ogundipe-Leslie's argument provides an important basis for my discussion of *Our Sister Killjoy* (hereafter *OSK*), *Americanah*, and *A Bit of Difference* (hereafter *ABD*). First, her analysis links African women's presence in the literary canon to the reclaiming of women's voices—an idea that is central to my argument. Second, her call for an explicitly "Third World" perspective is critically linked with transnational feminists' emphasis on comparative analysis of oppression, especially in the light of the growing influence of neoliberalism. A transnational feminist critique requires a reading or representational praxis that emphasizes both a "rooting" in specific histories and a "'shift' from . . . centers" (Collins, 2009: 265). Perhaps, this transnational aesthetic allows Aidoo, Adichie, and Atta to produce black African female characters whose voices run counter to hegemonic forces and discourses that transcend the local. As subsequently argued, Sissie, Ifemelu, and Deola are able to speak (and be heard) because of the unique perspectives that they form as they move through varied spaces and borders. Within this larger transnational context, these characters' status as "outsider[s] within" (Collins, 1986: s14) opens space for the subaltern [as woman and African] to *speak* and the global reader cannot help but *listen*.

TRANSNATIONAL FEMINIST AESTHETICS AND THE SELECTED TEXTS

This argument is situated within the "transnational turn" in literary criticism and the questions it raises about the complicated links between globalization and postcoloniality (Jay, 2010: 1–14). Also critical is Richards' (2000) observation that transnational literary feminism re-engages the "politics vs. aesthetics" debate that often characterizes Third World literary criticism and "affirms" subaltern voices (151). This perspective inspires analysis that considers literary aesthetics as a tool for sociopolitical critique that highlights African women's multilayered exploration of subalternity and their nuanced visions of gendered subaltern agency. Regarding Ogundipe-Leslie's Third World positionality, it is crucial that Mohanty's (2003) critical trajectory moves from "Third World Feminisms"—characterized by "critique" of misrepresentations in hegemonic discourses—to "Transnational Feminism"—characterized by "reconstruction" that envisions a "feminism without borders," which opens an epistemic space for building alliances that interrogate global oppression (221–234). This shift presents a new politics in which Global Southern women are not presented merely as victims but as critical voices in the process of imagining a more just world.

While my argument seemingly privileges mobility as a critical dimension of the diasporic impulses in African women's layered critique of oppression, this effort does not discount other (transnational) strategies that African women writers use to "write back" not only to the problematic (nationalist) discourses of African male authors but also the metanarratives of empire. Pinto's (2013) rethinking of "diaspora" as "a critical feminist category" (5) is essential for theorizing diaspora beyond mobility and considering "how a set of aesthetic and interpretive strategies" unite what might appear as incompatible spaces and times (4). Mobility per se is not the central concern here; rather, mobility forms part of a broader aesthetic form in which African women's voicing acquires transnational resonance. This critical mode, as Pinto claims, demands a different politics of reading African women's writings with implications for analyzing the "pinnacle of intersectional difficulty" engendered by African women's subaltern positionality (5 and 177).

Since transnational feminism became a buzzword only from the 1990s onwards, it is critical that its features are evident in *OSK* (1977), which—unlike *Americanah* (2013) and *ABD* (2013/2015)—is a much older text, suggesting that earlier African women's writings had this transnational sensibility. Besides a motif of travel, the selected texts' "anticapitalist transnational feminist practice" (Mohanty, 2003: 230) imbues them with political significance, providing a broader outlook on the complex workings of patriarchy. By foregrounding the local (micro) and global (macro) co-constitutiveness, the texts' transnational aesthetic praxes unravel possibilities for exploring intricate interconnections between individual identities and larger global politics with its attendant "scattered hegemonies" (Grewal and Kaplan, 1994: 7).

If the transnational element is critical in contemporary African women's writing, it is because Third World subjects—and by implication, African female authors—are already situated at the confluence of multiple translocalities so that even when their writings are set in "local" or indigenous contexts, they are likely to have transnational echoes. These subjective positionalities also imply that the characters in African women's writing, as Zulfiqar (2016) argues, "are negotiating identities which are neither essentialized nor unified but rather multiple" (12).

This subjective complexity is explored in the selected texts through transcontinental mobility, contextual reconfiguration, and hybridity. *OSK* focuses on Sissie's travel to Europe, highlighting the politics of mobility and what it suggests about the limits of liberal globalist emancipatory projects. In *Americanah,* Ifemelu, who was born and raised in Lagos, migrates to the United States for education, returning to Nigeria after 13 years. Her experiences abroad, and those of her classmates, complicate American racial politics by centering the unique experience of African migratory subjects without ignoring their links with the African American experience. In *ABD,* Deola, who works with the international charity organization LINK, was born in Ikoyi, an ex-colonial town in Nigeria, and educated in England. Through Deola's work—which takes her to places like Atlanta, New Delhi, and Nigeria—readers become privy to the politics and ethics of global humanitarian work and its problematic rhetorics. When Aidoo's *OSK* is read together with Atta's *ABD* and Adichie's *Americanah*, two different narratives of African migratory histories emerge; however, despite temporal differences, little has changed about the racialized receptions of black corporeal mobilities in the metropole.

The transcontinental mobility of the three texts engenders hybrid subjectivities, stressing how flows of people and cultures facilitate translocal crossings and accelerate transnational imaginings (Appadurai, 1996: 4). The hybridity resulting from this local-global fusion results in binary thinking and politics. In *ABD,* there is no "adequate description" of Deola's status: Deola insists that she is Nigerian but she sounds "British" and possesses a British passport (5). When Ifemelu, in *Americanah*, returns to Nigeria, her employer calls her "*a real American*. Ready to work, a no-nonsense person" (483). In *OSK*, hybridity is even evident in the text's multidiscursive poetics, including the subversion of the generic expectations of Western travel narratives. Aidoo's engagement with Conrad's *Heart of Darkness* (1971/1899) implies that *OSK* is always already caught up in transnational reading politics. If, as Hoeller (2004) argues, "*Our Sister Killjoy* gains its central drama from the haunting presence of Conrad's text" (141), one can argue that Aidoo's narrative is politically efficacious only within a transnational reading mode.

Despite their liminalities, the three character's postcolonial subjectivity shapes their engagement with the worlds around them. All three characters return home to continental Africa—a motif that points to the significance of situatedness even in a so-called postmodern world. While postmodernism emphasizes the fragmentation of identity, the portrayal of these characters suggests the continuing relevance of difference. These characters may be deemed "Afropolitan[s]" (Selasi, 2005)—perhaps not Sissie, who does not remain abroad long enough to be assimilated and whose politics is too radical for neoliberal cooptation, but they do not feel at "home" in the West. Ifemelu perceived Nigeria as the "only place" she "could sink her roots in without the constant urge to tug them out and shake off the soil" (Adichie, 2013: 7). Sissie's return to Ghana "felt like fresh honey on the tongue"; Ghana (and Africa) was "home" despite "its uncertainties" (Aidoo, 1977: 133). Deola has a complicated relationship with Nigeria for though she was "eager to leave Lagos" after her travel there, she misses it once she returns to London (Atta, 2013/2015: 204). She considers her stay in London after her Lagos trip as "a voluntary exile" and as the narrator suggests, she "will miss her flat" but not London when she returns to Nigeria, which she calls "home" (204).

MOBILITY AND GAZE

In all three narratives, mobility not only makes the protagonists aware of the power of the gaze but also results in the development of oppositional consciousness and subaltern agency. In opposition to postmodernist perspectives, mobility in these texts does not loosen but reveals the links between corporeality and difference. Sissie's awareness of the colonized/colonizer power relations is obvious when *OSK* opens. However, she is still politically immature when she arrives in Frankfurt for she seems to have been quickly taken in by the fetish-like qualities of the symbols of capitalism: "she walked . . . *looking, feasting* her village eyes" on shiny "Consumer Goods" (12). Ironically, as Sissie gazes at consumer objects, her bodily presence is othered in the Western space she finds herself. Sissie's oppositional consciousness begins to fully develop when she hears a woman calling her "das Schwartze Mädchen" (12, "black girl"), an incident that enlightens her about the power dimensions of the racialized gaze.

Having been *othered* during her transnational experiences, Sissie recognizes that the Western gaze is not innocent for it sets one group of humans against another. Sissie's encounter with the gaze causes her to also "other" through an intense reverse gaze on white bodies lumped together as nauseating "pickled pig parts" (12–13). However, Sissie's subaltern positionality allows her to recognize her gaze as immoral for "she was ashamed of her reaction" and "For the rest of her life, she was to regret this moment/when she was made to notice differences in human colouring" (12–13). Sissie's reaction confirms Mohanty's (2003) argument that privileging marginalized perspectives provides an expansive view of power and enables us to "envision [a more] just and democratic society" (231–232).

In a transnational mode, Aidoo links Sissie's singular experience to the larger problem of imperial racism. The narratorial commentary directly following this incident highlights how "any kind of difference" becomes a rationale for the (neo)colonial enterprise, which entails more than the grabbing of resources—such as land and oil—for it is shaped by "necropolitics"—to cite Mbembe (2016/2019): that is, the "Power to decide/Who is to live,/Who is to die" (13).

Even more significant is the "affective aesthetic" (see Schultermandl et al., 2018: 14–20) that underlies Aidoo's representation of Sissie's experiences. Sissie's affective and somatic responses—including rage, sadness, disdain—often punctuate the narrative. When Sissie was identified as a "black girl" in Germany, she felt a range of emotions: not only did she feel the urge "to vomit," she was also ashamed, "Something pulled inside of her," and she was remorseful (Aidoo, 1977: 12–13). The subaltern conditions in London made Sissie "[s]o sad she wanted to cry. And sometimes she . . . wept" (89). Besides Sissie's reactions to her experiences in the first three sections of the text, affect is also crucial in the final section "A Love Letter" where Sissie's quotidian discourse is set apart from the obvious stylistic experimentation in the rest of the narrative. Readers are hailed by Sissie's "affective interpellation[s]" (Schultermandl et al., 2018: 13), engendering a public affective response to [neo]colonial oppression. Hence, affect in Aidoo's transnational aesthetics is political.

ABD opens with Deola's arrival at the Atlanta airport where she sees the image of an African woman in a charity advertisement:

> The great ones capture you. This one is illuminated and magnified. It is a photograph of an African woman with desert terrain behind her. She might be

Sudanese or Ethiopian. It is hard to tell. Her hair is covered with a yellow scarf and underneath her image is a caption: "I Am Powerful." (Atta, 2013/2015: 1)

Deola's gaze and subsequent reaction foreground the power behind visual representations of the bodies of Third World women in humanitarian discourse. She contemplates: "I am powerful. . . . What does that mean? Powerful enough to grab the attention of a passerby, no doubt" (1). Through Deola's reaction, Atta draws readers' attention to the (un)ethical dimensions of global humanitarian efforts, indicating how the visuality of the African woman's photograph "others" and homogenizes African female subjectivity. This "spectacular rhetoric" has affective implications because it "frames" the subaltern "as an object of feeling and sight" (Hesford, 2011: 3). Significantly, it is impossible to tell whether the woman in the image is Sudanese or Ethiopian. Deola's contemplations show how the specific identity of the African woman becomes inconsequential as she is commodified for humanitarian purposes.

Deola's reflections on whether the woman has been sufficiently paid also denote what Grewal (2006) calls the "conjunction of geopolitics and biopolitics" (3) in the objectification of African female bodies in transnational charity projects. Deola "wince[s]" when she "imagines posters with the prime minister at Number Ten and the president in the Oval Office with the same caption underneath" (Atta, 2013/2015: 1). Although Deola works with an NGO—and is therefore complicit in a larger oppressive system—she is not uncritical of her work, often wondering what people thought of her job. Deola's response above underscores her ability to recognize and feel subaltern positionalities despite her own (limited) privileged status.

When *Americanah* opens, Ifemelu is waiting for the train—itself a symbol of mobility, setting the tone for an exploration of the connection between movement, difference, and corporeality. It is through Ifemelu's cross-spatial mobilities that readers become aware of black bodies as marked signifiers of a spatiocorporeal structure: "It startled her [Ifemelu], what a difference a few minutes of train travel made" (Adichie, 2013: 6). When Ifemelu rode public transport on her visits to Aunt Uju, it struck her that "mostly slim white people" alighted in Manhattan while those heading toward Brooklyn were "mostly black and fat" (6), hinting at the links between race, space, and class. Ifemelu's mobilities also take her to upper-middle-class spaces where she builds relationships with people like Curt—her rich white ex-boyfriend—and Blaine, her "bourgie" African American ex-boyfriend. Through these encounters, Ifemelu develops "her own new American selves" (235), learns about the workings of hegemonic power and comes to "gaze" at white Americans who talk about their "safari in Tanzania" or donations to charities "that built wells, a wonderful orphanage in Botswana, a wonderful microfinance cooperative in Kenya" (209).

It is through such mobilities that Ifemelu appreciates the indignities that come with being from a country that "received" and not "the country of people who gave . . . who had and could therefore bask in the grace of having given, to be among those who could afford to give copious pity and empathy" (209). Here, affective disposition is presented as a kind of dividend for humanitarian investment, pointing to relations of power and powerlessness between Ifemelu and the other privileged characters she encounters. Ifemelu's positionality as a Third World person takes her across spaces occupied by people from the Global South, like the African hair braiding salon, Aunt Uju's home, and the African Student Association, where she (and the reader) gain insight into varied immigrant experiences and struggles. In the African hair braiding salon, where Ifemelu is located as much of the narrative is told in flashbacks, Adichie explores another instantiation of the connections between spaces, corporeality, and difference.

OPPOSITIONAL CONSCIOUSNESS AND VOICING

The oppositional consciousness that the characters develop as they move is manifested through voicing. In *OSK*, the connection between oppositional consciousness and voicing becomes apparent when Sissie writes a love letter—on a return flight to Accra—in which she recounts her meeting with her "brothers." Here, Sissie's direct voice and perspective take over from the narratorial voice in her letter to her "Precious Something" (Aidoo, 1977: 115) because, as Odamtten (1994) suggests, she has matured politically from her experiences in Europe and thus cannot be silent (119 and 130). Connected to this is the crucial relation established between voicing and language at the beginning of Sissie's letter: "Since so far, I have only been able to use a language that enslaved me, and therefore, the messengers of my mind always come shackled?" (112). Sissie's imagery emphasizes the psychological and material violence of imperial language politics underlining the continued impact of this linguistic violence in her (and her people's) present postcolonial predicament for, as she argues, strangers are "watching and listening" in on their conversations about their "hopes . . . fears and . . . fantasies" (116 and 115). Sissie proposes a "secret language" (116) that enables the articulation of the postcolonial predicament without fear and forges liberatory futures that entail the building of new memories defined not by the wounds of imperialism but rather a new discourse of love and intimacy.

Unlike her brothers who are lost and prefer to stay in alien spaces, Sissie possesses a "righteous anger" perceived as "negative," "radical," or "so serious" (121 and 112–113) and through her letter, Sissie speaks back, sometimes in the form of curses that give rhetorical force to her critique of oppressive regimes: "A curse on all those who steal continents!" (120). Sissie's voicing emphasizes the African predicament, but she is careful not to reproduce the simplistic binaries that enable oppression: "Of course, we are different. No we are not better than anybody else" (116). The choice to speak through the mode of a love letter, which Sissie is "never going to post" (133), is itself rhetorically significant because epistolary enunciation—described "as a performative act of identity-formation" (Simon-Martin, 2015: 51)—enables Sissie to undertake a discursive action that affirms her subjectivity. The reciprocity of the epistolary form (Altman, 1982: 88) ensures that though Sissie's lover will not read the letter, the reader is interpellated and thus hears the voice of the subaltern. The intimacy of the epistolary form is itself a crucial dimension of the affective aesthetics in Aidoo's transnational feminism.

In *ABD*, Deola's voicing is not as caustic as those of Sissie and Ifemelu but it is equally critical of oppression. Because of her oppositional consciousness, Deola is considered a "radical," "the négritude sister" by her siblings (Atta, 2013/2015: 57). In conversations with her co-worker, Deola holds back her opinion because she does not want her views to be reduced to "the African woman's perspective" (10). This should not be construed as silence but as an effort to rhetorically control her narrative. Deola seems ambivalent especially at the beginning of the novel perhaps because, unlike Sissie and Ifemelu, she is directly implicated in coloniality through her job. She is not unaware of the privileges that come with her own middle-class status and the implications of working within an industry that thrives on the vulnerability of her continent. Deola eventually critiques her organization for its vetting policies—an action her co-worker calls "a gross betrayal" (207). By the end of the narrative, Deola seems even more critical. While watching a Hollywood movie about genocide in a fictional African country, she notices the movie's reproduction of Western salvationist rhetorics. Deola's response reflects her critical maturity because, unlike previous times, she refuses to be "seduced" by such a discourse (213). Deola is not dismissive of Africa's problems but "she has never recognized [the] Africa" in these misrepresentations (213). Deola's refusal to partake in these hegemonic viewing practices "speaks back" at such misrepresentations.

In *Americanah*, blogging is used to interrogate oppression and voice alternative narratives of race that may otherwise be silent. The story of how Ifemelu started blogging is illuminating. When her boyfriend Curt describes *Essence as* "racially skewed" (Adichie, 2013: 364), Ifemelu takes him to a bookstore—a kind of field trip—to educate him about racialized discrimination in beauty magazines. It is after this incident that Ifemelu emails Wambui, her friend, who encourages her to "start a blog," describing the email as "so raw and true" (366). Through this performative power of blogging, Ifemelu voices subaltern experiences for as one commentator indicates: "You've used your irreverent . . . thought provoking voice to create a space for real conversations about an important subject" (5). Before this incident with Curt, Ifemelu chose "silence" whenever she felt racially slighted (364). Blogging is not the only means by which Ifemelu "speaks" back. Dropping her American accent is also a symbolic act of voicing her oppositional consciousness for this action "returned her [Ifemelu's] voice to herself" (221).

COMPARATIVE PERSPECTIVE ON OPPRESSION

The three texts critique oppression in its myriad forms through an analysis of the complex intersections between race, gender, migration, and class. Each narrative extends its purview beyond the nation-state, allowing for more comparative perspectives on oppression. Indeed, the protagonists' voicing will not be effectual if it cannot engage with other subaltern experiences.

In *OSK*, Sissie's "black-eyed squint" is critical of oppression everywhere and in any form, including (neo)colonialism in Africa, the holocaust, apartheid, and slavery. The exploration of subalternity is so comprehensive: it forces us to see the connectedness of African diasporic experiences and those of other Third Worlders—for example, Indians, Philippinos, and Brazilians (Aidoo, 1977: 29–32). By subverting the colonial travel narrative, with its white male archetypal subject, and privileging the experiences of Sissie, Aidoo foregrounds the layered oppression of [post]colonial heteropatriarchy and the (im)possibilities of transnational coalition, made evident by the Sissie-Marija friendship for example.

Sissie shares a different history from Marija but through their complicated friendship, albeit tainted by a history of colonialism, she becomes privy to the gendered, racialized, and class oppression within the colonial space of Germany. In Sissie's epiphanic moment ("Suddenly Sissie knew," 65) following Marija's sexual advances, there is a recognition that the loneliness Marija feels is, like colonialism, a dimension of the injuries of modernity with the implication that both women's experiences are structured by heterocapitalism. In fact, Aidoo establishes a link between the colonial foundations of the German Third Reich (symbolized by the German castles, 69) and oppressive regimes in her African backyard (e.g., the Abomey Kings of Dahomey, 37), but Marija's links with colonial history are also reinforced by the fact that she is the wife/mother of Big/Little Adolf. It is Sissie's borderland identity as a black body in transit that makes these connections possible. This comparison interrogates the binarism often established between African literature that "write[s] back" and those about "the self" (Eze, 2016: 1–42) for Aidoo's critical praxis straddles between these two modes, highlighting the ways in which transnational aesthetics complicates literary analysis of power.

While Sissie's affective reactions empathize with Marija, her Pan-African outlook limits her responses. Sissie "felt pain" when she saw Marija's tear, but she also, subsequently, questions her own affective response toward Marija's circumstance: "Why weep for them" (66). Sissie's reaction is motivated by the fact that Marija, just as the Welsh lady she meets in London, is not a "soul sister" because of "her color/—and our history" (93). Unfortunately, Sissie's relations with her brothers are also fraught with problems. While Sissie goes to London to "compare notes" with her brothers (80), her meeting suggests that the possibilities for coalition are closed as it is clear that the brothers have become enamored by the promises of the metropole. Sissie's brothers, who perceive her as "so serious" (112), are complicit in the [neo]colonial oppressive regime that she critiques. The "intertextual dialogue" between Aidoo's narrative and African male writing suggests that "from Sissie's point of view, the African woman represents the wretchedness of Frantz Fanon's 'wretched of the earth'" (Owusu, 1990: 357). Underlying *OSK*'s comparative framing is therefore a representation of the dilemma of Third World feminism itself.

Americanah provides readers with a complex narrative of African migratory experience, while reflecting the experiences of other subaltern groups. Through Ifemelu's experiences and her engagement with other characters in the story, readers become aware of the diversities and similarities of African migratory experiences. The fact that parts of the novel happen in a flashback in the African hair braiding salon is crucial because Ifemelu's experiences in the United States are presented against the backdrop of the women's lives in the salon, which brings into proximity the First (their physical location) and Third (their now imagined homeland) Worlds. The salon is itself a gendered space where women speak about their experiences; however, such comparative engagements highlight Ifemelu's privileged status and the nuances of African subalternity.

Elsewhere, Ifemelu's "outsider within" (Collins, 1986) status allows her to critique the "simplistic comparison" (Adichie, 2013: 208) in Laura's observations about a "wonderful" African woman who did not get along with the African American in her graduate class because "She didn't have all those issues" (207). Ifemelu brings her attention to the nuances of black subalternities: "May be when the African American's father was not allowed to vote because he was black, the Ugandan's father was running for parliament or studying at Oxford" (207). In a transnational mode, Adichie points to "the trauma of trying to get an American visa" (173) that many internationals share and uses Ifemelu's (and other character's) struggles abroad as a basis for an anticapitalist critique. For instance, the micropolitics of capitalist violence is concretized when Ifemelu's financial difficulties lead her to desperation and she falls prey to sexual abuse, signifying the precarious position of females and Third World bodies in transit.

ABD is as much about the complexities of life in Nigeria as it is about the complexities of global humanitarianism. Deola's work at an international

NGO provides a means for exploring new oppressive regimes under contemporary globalism. In fact, two chapters are titled "Foreign Capitals" and "The Business of Humanitarianism." Here, Atta (2013/2015) untangles the politics and ethics of humanitarian work through Deola's engagement with Nigerian NGOs and her office in London. Deola's perspectives not only interrogate the mismatch between the needs of NGOs on the ground and the focus of international charity organizations but also point to the problematic rhetorics that charities use to evoke sympathy. When her colleague uses this kind of rhetoric in discussing HIV/AIDS in Africa, Deola reflects: "It makes her sad . . . too scared to dwell on how much Africa suffers" (148). When LINK ignores the recommendations from her visit to NGOs in Nigeria, Deola is willing to resign from the organization "if they can't be open to an idea that involves a community of Africans being independent" (152).

CONCLUSION

This paper has shown that the transnational feminist impulses in the selected texts do not only destabilize problematic images of African women but also highlight the efforts of African female writers to envision new representational politics that *unsilences* the subaltern. The transnational becomes an aesthetic that imagines a cosmopoetic praxis of subaltern representation and analysis—one that accounts for the salience of specific histories and experiences at the intersection of multiple forces and influences. By presenting African females as speaking subjects, privileging their perspectives and projecting them as the moral centers of their fiction, these authors create a rhetorical structure that subverts hegemonic discourses about African women as powerless and silent. Essentially, these works are radical political acts that interrogate the relations between alterity and larger global politics and are thus a means through which a transnational feminist vision is fulfilled. While there exists a strong link between mobility and subaltern voicing in the analysis, this chapter's notion of a transnational aesthetic is broader, including the emphasis on affect and comparative critique, which not only calls for a different politics of reading but also a broader literary analysis of power that moves beyond self/other, national/transnational binarisms.

REFERENCES

Adichie, Chimamanda Ngozi. 2013. *Americanah*. New York: Anchor Books.
Aidoo, Ama Ata. 1977. *Our Sister Killjoy*. London: Longman.

Altman, Janet Gurkin. 1982. *Epistolarity: Approaches to a Form*. Columbus: Ohio State University Press.
Appadurai, Arjun. 1996. *Modernity al Large: Cultural Dimensions of Globalization*. Minneapolis and London: University of Minnesota Press.
Atta, Sefi. 2013/2015. *A Bit of Difference*. Northampton, MA: Interlink Publishing.
Busia, Abena P. A. 1989. "Silencing Sycorax: On African Colonial Discourse and the Unvoiced Female." *Cultural Critique* (Winter): 81–104. https://www.jstor.org/stable/1354293.
Collins, Patricia Hill. 1986. "Learning from the Outsider Within: The Sociological Significance of Black Feminist Thought." *Social Problems* 33.6 (October–December): s14–s32. https://www.jstor.org/stable/800672.
Collins, Patricia Hill. 2009. *Black Feminist Thought: Knowledge, Consciousness, and the Politics of Empowerment*. New York and London: Routledge.
Conrad, Joseph. 1971/1899. *Heart of Darkness*. New York: Norton.
Cornell, Drucilla. 2010. "The Ethical Affirmation of Human Rights: Gayatri Spivak's Intervention." In *Can the Subaltern Speak? Reflections on the History of an Idea*, edited by Rosalind C. Morris, 100–116. New York: Columbia University Press.
Davies, Carol Boyce. 1986. "Introduction: Feminist Consciousness and African Literary Criticism." In *Ngambika: Studies of Women in African Literature*, edited by Carol Boyce Davies and Anne Adams Graves, 1–24. Trenton: African World Press.
Davies, Carole Boyce, and Elaine Savory Fido. 1993. "African Women Writers: Toward a Literary History." In *A History of Twentieth Century African Literatures*, edited by Oyekan Owomoyela, 311–346. Lincoln, Nebraska and London: University of Nebraska Press.
Eze, Chielozona. 2016. *Ethics and Human Rights in Anglophone African Women's Literature: Feminist Empathy*. Cham, Switzerland: Springer.
Grewal, Inderpal. 2006. *Transnational America: Feminisms, Diasporas, Neoliberalisms*. Durham and London: Duke University Press.
Grewal, Inderpal, and Caren Kaplan. 1994. "Introduction: Transnational Feminist Practices and Questions of Postmodernity." In *Scattered Hegemonies: Postmodernity and Transnational Feminist Practices*, edited by Inderpal Grewal and Caren Kaplan, 1–33. Minneapolis: University of Minnesota Press.
Hesford, Wendy. 2011. *Spectacular Rhetorics: Human Rights Visions, Recognitions, Feminisms*. Durham and London: Duke University Press.
Hoeller, Hildegard. 2004. "Ama Ata Aidoo's *Heart of Darkness*." *Research in African Literatures* 35.1 (Spring): 130–147. https://www.jstor.org/stable/3821407.
Jay, Paul. 2010. *Global Matters: The Transnational Turn in Literary Studies*. Ithaca and London: Cornell University Press.
Maggio, Jay. 2007. "'Can the Subaltern Be Heard?': Political Theory, Translation, Representation, and Gayatri Chakravorty Spivak." *Alternatives* 32.4 (October): 419–443. https://doi.org/10.1177/030437540703200403.
Mbembe, Achille. 2016/2019. *Necropolitics*. Durham and London: Duke University Press.

Mohanty, Chandra Talpade. 2003. *Under Western Eyes: Decolonizing Theory, Practicing Solidarity*. Durham, NC: Duke University Press.
Newell, Stephanie. 2006. *West African Literatures: Ways of Reading*. New York: Oxford University Press.
Odamtten, Vincent O. 1994. *The Art of Ama Ata Aidoo: Polylectics and Reading Against Neocolonialism*. Gainesville: University Press of Florida.
Ogundipe-Leslie, Molara. 1994. *Re-Creating Ourselves: African Women & Critical Transformations*. Trenton, NJ: Africa World Press.
Owusu, Kofi. 1990. "Canons Under Siege: Blackness, Femaleness, and Ama Ata Aidoo's Our Sister Killjoy." *Callaloo* 13.2 (Spring): 341–363. https://www.jstor.org/stable/2931711.
Pinto, Samantha. 2013. *Difficult Diasporas: The Transnational Feminist Aesthetic of the Black Atlantic*. New York: New York University Press.
Richards, Constance S. 2000. *On the Winds and Waves of Imagination: Transnational Feminism and Literature*. New York and London: Garland Publishing Inc.
Sandoval, Chela. 1991. "US Third World Feminism: The Theory and Method of Oppositional Consciousness in the Postmodern World." *Genders* 10 (Spring): 1–24. https://doi.org/10.5555/gen.1991.10.1.
Schultermandl, Silvia, Katharina Gerund, and Anja Mrak. 2018. "The Affective Aesthetics of Transnational Feminism." *WiN: The EAAS Women's Network Journal* 1: 1–23. WiN: The EAAS Women's Network Journal Issue 1 (2018)—European Association for American Studies Women s Network.
Selasi, Taiye. 2005. Bye-Bye Barbar (Or What is an Afropolitan). *The Lip Magazine*, March 3. http://thelip.robertsharp.co.uk/?p=76.
Simon-Martin, Meritxell. 2015. "Barbara Leigh Smith Bodichon's Travel Letters: Performative Identity-Formation in Epistolary Narratives." In *Performing the Self: Women's Lives in Historical Perspective*, edited by Katie Barclay and Sarah Richardson, 49–62. London and New York: Routledge.
Spivak, Gayatri Chakravorty. 1994/1985. "Can the Subaltern Speak?" In *Colonial Discourse and Postcolonial Theory: A Reader*, edited by Patrick Williams and Laura Chrisman, 66–109. New York: Columbia University Press.
Stratton, Florence. 1994. *Contemporary African Literature and the Politics of Gender*. NewYork: Routledge.
Zulfiqar, Sadia. 2016. *African Women Writers and the Politics of Gender*. Newcastle upon Tyne: Cambridge Scholars Publishing.

Chapter 6

Local and Global Perspectives on Nigerian Women's Activism in *News from Home* by Sefi Atta

Rose A. Sackeyfio

Sefi Atta effectively conveys diverse experiences and challenges of diaspora life for African women in her short story collection *News from Home* (2010). As the central work in the collection, "*News from Home*" explores the tensions between local and global spaces in the lives of Nigerian women at home and abroad. Through a spatiotemporal nexus, this chapter interrogates the ways in which Sefi Atta's novella, "*News from Home*," foregrounds the perspective of the female protagonist whose experiences span Nigeria and the transnational setting of America. The collection contains ten short stories and among them "A Temporary Position" and "Green" explore transnational sites that include London and America. Sefi Atta's novel *A Bit of Difference* (2012) highlights the tensions between Nigeria as homeland and London in ways that that shape the life of a Nigerian woman.

Through an eco-feminist framework, this chapter also examines the relationship between the oppression of women and the destruction of the environment. Women's relationship to the earth is a salient theme within the cultural traditions of diverse African communities. In the Niger Delta, women's solidarity and organized protests draw upon indigenous traditions of resistance as the basis of Sefi Atta's fictional account of actual events in the twenty-first century. Atta skillfully positions the collision of environmental devastation in the Niger Delta and Nigerian women's activism through the perceptions of Eve, a female immigrant in the United States. The news the protagonist receives from her home in the Niger Delta highlights women's agency as a compelling theme. As the central piece in the collection, "*News from Home*" examines women's identity, hybridity, agency, and ecofeminism.

Atta is a leading Nigerian female playwright and author whose fiction explores important themes that arise in the global age of African migration and shifting perceptions of women's identity in the world. Atta is the winner of the 2006 Wole Soyinka Prize for Literature in Africa for her debut novel *Everything Good Will Come* (2006). She is also the winner of the coveted Noma Award for publishing in Africa in 2009. Her fiction is critically acclaimed and includes *Swallow* (2008), *A Bit of Difference* (2012), and her latest novel *The Bead Collector* (2019). Atta's talent and insight into the nature of diaspora landscapes captures the ethos of female subjectivity that firmly establishes her career as a leading writer of women's fiction today.

The contemporary genre of African diaspora literature represents the expansion of conventional themes and motifs that have characterized African women's writing since the first generation of female writers emerged in the mid-twentieth century to command new spaces in the African literary world till the present. Important themes during this period include patriarchy, traditional customs and practices, feminist consciousness, and the colonial encounter. Early African women writers who crafted fictional works with diaspora settings include Buchi Emecheta's London novels *In the Ditch* (1972) and *Second Class Citizen* (1974) and Ama Atta Aidoo's *Our Sister Killjoy: Or Reflections of a Black Eyed Squint* (1979). Although written in the twentieth century, these iconic works are linked inter-textually through the centrality of women protagonists that navigate the challenging experiences of *otherness* in the African diaspora. This body of works paved the way for women's literary voices to awaken in third-generation writers whose works are now celebrated in the African literary world and beyond.

Like her literary godmothers, Sefi Atta writes from a diaspora perspective to craft compelling fiction that interrogates twenty-first-century themes of hybridity, transnationalism, gender dynamics, feminism, race, class, among others in her short fiction and novels. "*News from Home*" represents Atta's engagement with African women's identity in new ways that contributes to an evolving tradition of women's writing that is transforming the African novel in subject and theme.

In the global age, African female authors that are based in the West are producing award-winning fiction that mirrors increasing migration of African people across borders, nationalities, and diverse ethno-linguistic spaces. Notable among these is Chimamanda Ngozi Adichie's *Americanah* (2013) and short story collection *The Thing Around Your Neck*. Chika Unigwe published *On Black Sisters' Street* in 2012 and in 2020 a collection of short fiction, *Better Late than Never*. Both works bring to life the stories of African immigrants who must re-negotiate their identities beyond Africa's borders. Ghanaian author, Taiye Selasie's widely acclaimed novel, *Ghana Must Go* (2013) is a vivid account of a Ghanaian family based in America who return to Ghana. No Violet Bulawayo's *We Need New Names* (2013) spans Zimbabwe and America to chronicle the coming of age tale of a young female protagonist. Yaa Gyasi is a gifted writer from Ghana whose sprawling work of historical fiction, *Homegoing* (2016) spans seventeenth-century Ghana, the Antebellum south in America, and the twenty-first century. The women characters in all of the works evolve a strong measure of agency and feminist consciousness that re-defines African womanhood. Finally, the works represent new directions in the African novel through diverse perspectives on shifting constructions of identity for African women at home and abroad.

Salient features that appear within *News from Home* parallel events that are ripped from the Nigerian and International headlines throughout the twenty-first century to spotlight the environmental crisis in the Niger Delta. The woman at the center of the work is Eve, and although she is a trained nurse, she migrates to New Jersey to be the nanny in the home of a Nigerian couple who are both doctors. The work is a rich tapestry of culture shock and conflicting realities in America that is finely sketched against the background of women's activism in her hometown in Nigeria.

The story unfolds in flashbacks that move the reader from the past to the present. Feminist consciousness awakens at the individual and communal level as Eve reflects upon her future, the environmental crisis, and growing activism of women in her community. The spatiotemporal dimensions of the work profile the female character whose diaspora life unfolds contradictions and uncertainty in America. The news the protagonist receives from her home in the Niger Delta highlights women's agency as a central theme. Through recollections of the protagonists' life in Nigeria, the work is a chronicle of the destructive impact of oil extraction on the social and economic life of her community through a gendered lens.

Eve migrates to New Jersey where her Nigerian identity is contested under troubling circumstances as a nanny for a Nigerian couple. She arrives in America without a green card and no legal status to be employed. Like most women she left behind in her community, she is frustrated by unemployment, the bleak conditions caused by environmental devastation, and unfortunately, a life made worse by a failed romance. The marginalized nature of her life makes the prospect of becoming a live-in nanny in America sound appealing. When she was younger she thought, "going to America was as fantastic as going to heaven" (Atta, 2010: 187). Although she has a nursing degree, the socioeconomic conditions in her hometown make unemployment a norm.

After being rejected for a nursing job with Summit Oil, Eve observes "Most nurses she graduated with were selling bottled water, bathing soap, tinned milk for a living" (Atta, 2010: 171). The harsh economic circumstances that women face are illustrated through the ill-fated experience of Amen, a young woman in Eve's community who is unmotivated to attend nursing school. She tells Eve, "But look at you, Eve. Since you graduated, you have no job" (Atta, 2010: 180). Later on, Amen turns to prostitution and becomes a member of the Better Life Brothel in Port Harcourt, eventually arrested by the Naval Police. Eve observes, "Prostitutes with a college education had better chances of finding expatriate customers who would keep them" (Atta, 2010: 184).

Despite the deplorable circumstances for women in the Niger Delta, Atta skillfully interweaves the leadership of a strong woman character named Madam Queen who emerges to ignite women's solidarity in defense of their environment. As Eve hears news of women's evolving activism, her employer remarks: "it is good that women are involved this time. Women, we are always the first affected and the last to be heard" (Atta 189). In *"News from Home,"* the "unsilencing" of women evokes feminist consciousness as women break free of their muted voices to control their destiny and reclaim the land. Madam Queen becomes a leader who articulates the massive environmental crisis and economic degradation of her community. Eve recalls that "she is speaking against the oil companies" (Atta, 2010: 191). Madam Queen is a finely sketched character, described as "fearless" . . . "Just like a man" (Atta, 2010: 192).

Through a diaspora lens, Eve contemplates the complexities of women's identity in her homeland and recalls conventional norms for females such as silencing of women's voices. She describes herself as "not being fluent in silence like most women" she knew (Atta, 2010: 180). Her mother warns her about the virtues of keeping quiet, especially after she is married. The feminist impulse to speak out is an act of resistance for Eve as well as the women in the Niger Delta.

The women from Eve's community share a marginalized status and vulnerability to social, economic, and political forces beyond their control. From Eve's vantage point in the diaspora, she remains connected to their struggle to rise above environmental constraints. Before departing for America, Eve had begun to listen to Madam Queen as if she had "fallen under her spell" (Atta, 2010: 191), which sparks her interest in hearing "news from home."

Eve's impressions of life in America mirror the immigrant experience of culture shock as her new identity takes shape. Gradually, she comes of age to the disjointed and abrasive realities of racial *otherness* and un-belonging in America. She wonders whether living in America will be different for her as she navigates antagonistic realities such as new awareness of racial dynamics. Eve recalls:

> sometimes a shop assistant follows me in a store, and I want to turn and scream 'if not for the havoc your people have wreaked in my country, would I be here taking shit from you?!' Then, on a day like this, I think of the guerilla politicos in my country, petroleum hawkers who treat the land and the people of the Niger Delta like waste matter. (Atta, 2010: 182)

Eve experiences discomforting encounters when Americans ask where she is from and sometimes look at her suspiciously. Her Nigerian identity is subsumed as simply African because American's behave as if Africa is a country.

Eve's reflections on the status of women in the Niger Delta are juxtaposed with realities of gender roles of Nigerian women in the diaspora through encounters with her employer Dr. Darego, a medical doctor who is also from her community in the Niger Delta. Sefi Atta illustrates pressing issues that Nigerian women face both at home and abroad. In pairing immigrant women who are both from the Niger Delta, "*News from Home*" examines parallel features of their lives. Neither Dr. Darego nor Eve has acquired legal status in America. Dr. Darego's children tell Eve: "She's a doctor, but she hasn't got her papers, so she can't work yet" (Atta, 2010: 174). Dr. Darego confides to Eve that the reason she has no green card is because when she came to America, she included herself on her husband's visa. Likewise, Eve has secret plans to locate a green card sponsor so that she can work legally as a nurse. Another immigrant named Charity reminds her that she is working illegally for the Darego family who are breaking federal laws. Women's subjectivity is heightened and their predicament displays the irony of educated females that still face barriers to economic stability in both Nigeria and America.

Similar to the women in "*News from Home*," Atta skillfully pairs women characters in her earlier works such as *Everything Good Will Come*, where Enitan and Sherry are friends whose lives take different paths. Both women develop a strong sense of their identity, agency, and feminist awakening by the end of the work. Moreover, the novel *Swallow* portrays the challenges of survival in Lagos for Tolani and Rose. The women face poverty, sexual harassment, and undetermined futures as victims of economic hardship and lack of education. One of them meets an unfortunate end but her friend is empowered through a new sense of agency.

Eve's consciousness unfolds from the transnational perspective through reflection on life in America and news from Nigeria that spark her growing solidarity with the women back home. She makes constant comparisons between Nigeria and America, examines women's roles and develops strategies to chart her future. As a new immigrant, Eve makes many unfavorable and discomforting discoveries about America, especially through interactions in the Nigerian home where she is employed.

In her role as a nanny in the Darego household, Eve becomes aware of negative stereotypes of Africa through the distorted perceptions of Dr. Darego's children. They are thoroughly Americanized and unwittingly they reveal family secrets. When Eve meets them:

> their expressions were Who-are-you? and What-d' you want? Their accents were wanna, gonna, shoulda. . . . Daniel tells Eve: I sawed the picture of Africa.

... And the boy had no hair, and his belly was all swelled up, and he lived in a hut with, um no, windows and I don't like Africa. Africa women have droopy boobies. (2010: 174)

These perceptions represent the influence of the American environment on Nigerian identity as a byproduct of diaspora life. Mrs. Darego's parenting skills are weak and reflect a permissive approach to raising children that is common in much of the west. Her demanding life as a physician creates emotional and physical distance from her children. Her life is a balancing act between her family and her work that fuels the need for a live-in nanny. As a medical doctor, Mrs. Darego is similar to Ifemelu's Aunty Uju, who is also a physician in Chimamanda Ngozi Adiche's *Americanah*. Their roles are very similar in that both characters are weak and ineffective parents whose children develop identity issues and behavior problems in America. Eve learns more about the Darego's empty marriage when she overhears them quarreling, and they go their separate ways. Their son tells Eve: "My mom really wants her papers because my dad is controlling" (Atta, 2010: 175). These observations reveal the gender dynamics, but the shallow existence of an elite Nigerian family who at first glance appear to have achieved the American dream.

The year 2002 is a pivotal stage in Eve's journey to America because it is the same year that news from Nigeria makes headlines in the western media. "*News from Home*" is a vivid illustration of art imitating life because on July 14, 2002, the headlines read: "Nigerian Women in Peaceful Protest Shut Down Oil Plant" (Atta, 2010: 170). In *News from Home*, Eve listens to broadcasts from Nigeria and thinks to herself that:

Forty years it took for our story to reach the front pages of the *Times: Nigerian Delta Women in Oil Company Standoff.* The women had occupied Summit Oils Terminal, the report said. They were clapping and singing. If their demands were not met, they would strip naked, and this was a shaming gesture, according to local custom. (Atta, 2010: 170)

Ecofeminism represents a theoretical framework of feminist discourse within the Womanist traditions that evolved during the mid-1980s in Africa and the African diaspora. With reference to Atta's *News from Home*, ecofeminism draws upon the role of indigenous women's organizations, and strategies that are essentially feminist in nature, although they are not identified as such by local Nigerian or African communities of women. In defining the term ecofeminism, its origins date from 1974, credited to a French feminist, Francois d' Eaubonne and is based upon the relationship between the oppression of women and the environment ... and on the relationship between women, society and nature (Salman, 2010: 854). Further, Salman asserts that "women world wide are often the first ones to notice environmental degradation" (2010: 844–855). This is certainly the case in the Niger Delta, since women earn their livelihood through farming and fishing. Sustained environmental damage from oil extraction exacerbates the pitiable conditions for local communities with women cast to the bottom of the economic ladder. Anugwom emphasizes how "The Niger Delta region suffers pervasive poverty, with women being almost twice as much affected by poverty than men" (2001: 66). Eve learns that 150 women shut down most of a multinational oil company's operations for nearly a week. The unarmed women have occupied the terminal stopping exports and trapping about 700 workers inside (Atta). Bahati Kuumba in "African Women, Resistance Cultures and Cultural Resistances" states:

> The resilience of African women's culture of structural autonomy was demonstrated in July 2002 when women in the Delta region of Nigeria drew upon their associations and networks to challenge the power of transnational corporations. More than 200 women took over and occupied a US-based Chevron oil refinery and forced the corporate elites to address their list of demands. (2006: 114)

The protest eventually included up to 2000 women who demanded jobs for their husbands and children along with socio-economic benefits. They also protested environmental degradation and the destruction of farmlands and widespread pollution.

The protagonist recalls graphic details of the environmental devastation that lead to the women's protests:

> In my hometown we had rainbow-colored water. It tasted of the oil that had leaked into our well. Bathing water we fetched from a creek. This smelled of dead crayfish. Our rivers were also dead. When rain fell, it rusted rooftops, shriveled plants. People who drank rainwater swore that it burnt permanent holes in their stomachs. (Atta, 2010: 175–176)

Since oil was discovered in the region in 1958, local communities have experienced extreme poverty, disruption of their livelihoods, health hazards, and many social ills because of environmental damage caused by crude oil extraction. The oil-rich environment suffers the ravages of exploitation, abuse, and violence against the land and women are disproportionately affected. Ekine describes how:

> On many occasions, the spillages lead to raging fires, as the case of the Jesse fire (October 17, 1998) when more than a thousand people were killed and

thousands more were left homeless, many with horrendous burns. In a region where medical care is scarce and only available for the rich, it is easy to imagine what happened to these people. Ponds, creeks, rivers, and land are soaked with thick layers of oil. (2010: 236)

The ecological devastation, poverty, and health hazards have pushed the local population to the wall and women are the most vulnerable within a complex network of debilitating realities through dependence on farming and fishing for survival. Anugwom notes the ways in which "the destruction of the Niger Delta environment through oil extraction implies that women from the region suffer more socio-economic deprivation than the average woman from other parts of the country" (2007: 62).

Through flashbacks, Eve's recalls vivid images of damage caused by gas flares:

> The villages had perpetual daylight once the gas flaring started. The flare was where cassava farms used to be. Summit Oil bulldozed those farms and ran pipelines through them. The land was now sinking . . . from the center of town we could smell burning mixed with petrol. (Atta, 2010: 176)

The severe economic and environmental crisis has worsened over the last 15 years, exacerbated by reoccurring oil spills that damage farmlands and pollute rivers and streams that are vital sources of fresh drinking water and fishing as a major livelihood. The centrality of women's (dis) empowerment, in the Niger Delta and the political nature of their protests translates to feminist expressions of ecofeminism and to as a viable strategy of survival and empowerment. Eve, recollects her life back home, where she visited a hospital attending to people made ill by the environmental damage. She recollects:

> there were also patients with strange growths, chronic respiratory illnesses, terminal diarrhea, weeping sores, inexplicable bleeding. We had too many miscarriages in our town, stillbirths, babies dying in utero, women dying in labor. People blamed the gas flare. They came to the clinic and sat for hours. An old man, said to be over a hundred years old, states that: "The land was our mother, he said, and we would suffer for allowing foreigners to violate her." (Atta, 2010: 177)

This conflict has resulted in militant protests, massive grassroots mobilization, and the politics of negotiation. Edlyne Anugwom asserts that "women, just like other members of the Niger Delta region, are well aware of the domestic political and economic structures that are responsible for the condition of the delta" (2007: 62). This means that acute poverty and disenfranchisement is a breeding ground for marginalized people in general and women in particular to engage in political, social, and economic actions to address their deprivation. Although the women's protests have in fact resulted in a measure of concessions from transnational actors, the response has not been sustained in ways that significantly transform the lives of women and their communities in the Niger Delta. It is evident that in light of ecofeminism's reverence for the earth and indigenous cultural origins, it is no wonder that elements of these ideas emerge clearly in the behaviors and strategies of women's groups.

Ecofeminist activism dominates the events later in the novella when Madam Queen begins to organize the women for action through impassioned speeches about their ravaged communities:

> "The oil companies," she said, "they drill our fathers' farms and don't give us jobs. . . . There are no fish in our rivers, no bush rats left in our forest. We don't use natural gas in our homes and yet we have gas flares in our backyards. We can't find kerosene to buy and we have pipelines running through our land. Some of us don't have electricity." . . . Women listen to me. . . . As we speak we are dying. We are dying of our air, we are dying of our water. WE are dying from oil. Must we continue to stand by in silence and wait for men to fight our battles?' (Atta, 2010: 190–191)

Sokari Ekine's fieldwork in the Niger Delta is documented in "Women's Response to State Violence in the Niger Delta." In addition to severe economic devastation, women's activism is sparked by various forms of gendered violence. Ekine confirms:

> In the Niger Delta, women are both victims of violence and agents of resistance. Women in the Niger Delta channel their resistance into a variety of forms, including dancing and singing; collective action such as demonstrations and strikes; testimonies and silence; culturally significant responses, such as stripping naked; refusing to change work routines and habits, such as opening up market stalls or collecting water; participating in women's meetings; and struggling to maintain their daily routines amid the chaos and violence that surrounds them. Of the forms of resistance to violence, escape is considered the most extreme, as it is usually only ventured in dire circumstances. (2010: 23)

These types of resistance behaviors illustrate that women's collective activism in the Niger Delta has a long and deeply entrenched history in response to social and economic forces that threaten them and their livelihood.

Further, Eve recalls the tragic events surrounding the execution of Ken Saro Wiwa and others in Port Harcourt in 1995. When the Ogoni people protested against Shell oil, "Security forces came and shot at them, burned down their homes, beat up women and children. . . . Ken Saro Wiwa and others who led the movement were tried by a military tribunal and hanged" (Atta, 2010: 193). Saro Wiwa was a prominent environmental activist, author, and founder of the Movement for Survival of Ogoni People (MOSOP) in the Niger Delta. Hundreds of Ogoni were murdered under the military junta of General Sani Abacha (Adebajo et al., 1995: 472–474).

The story ends on a dramatic note as Eve contemplates her future in America. She and Dr. Darego learn through news broadcasts of the demonstrations in her hometown and she sees Madam Queen, her best friend, her Mother, and many other women that she recognizes among the activists.

Women's activism in the Niger Delta is not formally identified as a feminist movement. This was also true of the famed Aba Women's War of 1929, the Greenbelt Movement in Kenya, or the dynamic activism of Funmilayo Ransome-Kuti and her organization, the African Women's Union during the colonial period of the 1940s and 1950s. However, as these examples clearly illustrate, women's collective actions and the demand for social, economic, and political justice, intersect with other forms of oppression, environmental degradation notwithstanding. Women's collective responses to these forms of injustice and economic violence represent the basic tenets of feminism, regardless of the ideological proclivities of diverse nomenclature. Patriarchal structures of government, the oil companies, and the military collude to brutalize local communities through economic deprivation, and the massive failure to redress the pitiable conditions of impoverishment that challenge women's ability to survive and maintain their families and local communities.

Although there are many limitations to their effectiveness and success, Augustine Ikelegbe corroborates the traditional underpinnings, cultural moorings, communal nature, and flexibility of local women's groups as important strengths. Ikelegbe succinctly examines the ways in which indigenous "Women organizations, movements and groupings preceded colonialism" (2005: 249). In response to the environmental crisis, women's peaceful protests are characterized as "civil society response" (2005: 249). Moreover, Anugwom notes the importance of women in the Niger Delta narrative because "women have confronted the challenge of environmental degradation and the hardship in the farming and fishing communities of the delta as well as the escalating environmental politics in the region" (2007: 59). The women's demonstrations were in stark contrast to young militants who kidnap foreigners, carry weapons, and engage in violence. This illustrates a full measure of political consciousness by the women's organizations and is reminiscent of the anti-colonial sentiments and activism for independence from the colonial powers.

Furthermore, the strategies for women's activism draw upon other patterns of protest when women from different ethnic communities come together to demonstrate and protest. Ekine recalls the testimony of one of the women:

> The rivers they are polluting are our life and death. We depend on the rivers for everything. . . . When this situation became unbearable, we decided to come together to protest. Ijaw, Itsekiri, and Ilaje, we are one, we are brothers and sisters, it is only people who do not understand who think we are fighting ourselves. Our common enemies are the oil companies and their backers. (2010: 245)

This testimonial resonates a profound sense of agency and the interdependent relationship between the people and the environment. Moreover, the political and economic dimensions of the wanton destruction of the environment seem almost incomprehensible.

These behaviors of quiet protest are similar to Gandhi in India as well as the peaceful protest marches in the American south during the Civil Rights era. Further, Catherine Acholonu in *Motherism: The Afrocentric Alternative to Feminism* asserts the centrality of rural women as custodians of the earth through expression of the Female Principle. Her ideas resonate contemporary environmental activism, and she affirms that "for centuries indeed, the woman, like the earth has borne, nurtured, supported and protected humanity unnoticed, unpraised, unknown. But not anymore" (Acholonu, 1995: 119). These sentiments, rendered so poignantly, echo feminist energies that surface among the women in the Niger Delta.

In sum, ecofeminism represents a theoretical framework of feminist discourse within the womanist traditions that evolved during the mid-1980s in Africa and the African diaspora. Ecofeminism draws upon the role of indigenous women's organizations and strategies that are essentially feminist in nature, although they are not identified as such by local African communities of women.

Finally, in writing *News from Home*, Sefi Atta has turned life into art and presented realistic portrayals of women's agency, political consciousness, and environmental activism in the Niger Delta. The juxtaposition of the protagonists' harsh and confusing existence in America with a dark and uncertain future in the Niger Delta illustrates the vulnerability of women who are tossed about by forces they cannot control. The intersection of race, class, and gender subjectivity is a complex and dynamic matrix, but in the end both the protagonist and the women from her community in the Niger Delta take action to alleviate their plight. In New Jersey, Eve has formulated a plan to become independent of the couple she works for and the novella ends on a positive note of hope for a better life. Ecofeminism asserts the female principle in preserving and replenishing the environment and celebrates women's connection to the earth and to the survival of the human family. *News from Home* illuminates the ways in which women's lives are shaped by the social, political, economic, and physical environment they inhabit. Regardless of the environment, African women display resilience to meet the challenge to negotiate and re-define their identities in order to survive and succeed in life.

REFERENCES

Acholonu, Catherine. 1995. *Motherism: The Afrocentric Alternative to Feminism.* Nigeria: Afa Publications.
Adebajo, Olukoshi, et al. 1995. "A Tribute to Ken Saro-Wiwa." *Review of African Political Economy*, Vol. 22, No. 66, Dec. 471–480.
Adichie, Chimamanda Ngozi. 2009. *The Thing Around Your Neck.* Toronto: Alfred A. Knopf.
Adichie, Chimamanda Ngozi. 2013. *Americanah.* Toronto: Alfred A. Knopf.
Aidoo, Ama Ata. 1979. *Our Sister Killjoy: Or Reflections of a Black Eyed Squint.* Lagos/New York: Nok Press.
Anugwom, Edlyne. 2007. "Stuck in the Middle: Women and Struggle for Survival in the Oil-Degraded Niger Delta." *Agenda: Empowering Women for Gender Equity*, No. 73. Biopolitics: New Technologies Trilogy, Vol. 1. 58–68.
Atta, Sefi. 2005. *Everything Good Will Come.* Northampton: Interlink Books.
Atta, Sefi. 2010. *News from Home.* North Hampton: Interlink Books.
Atta, Sefi. 2011. *Swallow.* Northampton: Interlink Books.
Atta, Sefi. 2013. *A Bit of Difference.* Northampton: Interlink Books.
Atta, Sefi. 2019. *The Bead Collector.* Northhampton: Interlink Books.
Bulawayo, No Violet. 2013. *We Need New Names.* New York: Reagan Arthur Books, Little Brown Company.
Ekine, Sokari. 2010. "Women's Response to State Violence in the Niger Delta." In *African Women Writing Resistance: Contemporary Voices*, edited by Jennifer Browdy, et al. Madison: University of Wisconsin Press. 235–247.
Emecheta, Buchi. 1972. *In the Ditch.* London: Heineman.
Emecheta, Buchi. 1974. *Second Class Citizen.* New York: George Braziller.
Emecheta, Buchi. 1986. *Head Above Water.* London: Fontara.
Emecheta, Buchi. 1994. *Kehinde.* London: Heinemann.
Green, December. 1999. *Gender Violence in Africa: African Women's Responses.* New York: St. Martin's Press.
Ikelegbe, Augustine. 2005. "Engendering Civil Society: Oil, Women Groups and Resource Conflicts in the Niger Delta Region of Nigeria." *The Journal of Modern African Studies*, Vol. 43, No. 2. 241–270.
Kuumba, Bahati M. 2006. "African Women, Resistance Cultures and Cultural Resistances." *Agenda: Empowering Women for Gender Equity*, No. 68, Culture. 112–114.

Kuumba, Bahati M. 2013. "African Feminisms in Exile: Diasporan, Transnational and Transgressive." *Agenda: Empowering Women for Gender Equity*, No. 58, African Feminisms Three. 3–11.

Salman, Aneel, and Iqbal Nuzhat. 2007. "Ecofeminist Movements-from the North to the South." *The Pakistan Development Review*, Vol. 46, No. 4. 853–864.

Unigwe, Chika. 2009. *On Black Sisters Street*. London: Jonathan Cape.

Unigwe, Chika. 2019. *Better Late than Never*. Abuja/London: Cassava Shorts.

Chapter 7

Breaking Mythical Barriers through a Feminist Engagement with Magical Realism

Elijah Adeoluwa Olusegun

Magical Realism and/or fantasy narratives are underrepresented in the fiction of female writers, especially African women authors. Notable works by male writers such as Ben Okri's *The Famished Road* (1991), Ngugi wa Thiong'o's *Wizard of the Crow* (2008), and K. Sello Duiker's *The Hidden Star* (2011) denote magical realism in African narratives. These writers use their fiction to engage the African cultural, social, mythical, and political landscapes. Their fictive imaginations are deeply rooted in the religiocultural and sociopolitical environment that fuel their creativity. The ground-breaking novels of African American writer, Octavia Butler, who "uses her strange worlds to explore issues of race and gender from our own strange world" (Ratterman, 1991: 26), inspire emerging production of Afrofuturistic works by women. Butler's futuristic works such as *Kindred* (1979), *Dawn* (1987), *Adulthood Rite*s (1988) *Imago* (1989), *Parable of the Talents* (2003), and *Parable of the Sower* (2012) provide a context in which African female writers may engage with futuristic or science fiction themes that incorporate elements of black history and culture.

Unlike the well-established writers in African magical realism and fantasy fiction whose works are rooted in African mythological culture and folklore, Nnedi Okorafor emerges as a new voice from an African diaspora perspective and is influenced by both African and American myths—which enrich her works as her characters straddle different cultural space(s) to understand the cosmic realism of their existence. This chapter thus explores Okorafor's *Who Fears Death* (2010) and *What Sunny Saw in the Flames* (2011) as new engagements in organic fantasy.

Her narratives straddle both real and magical fantasy in a refreshingly engaging manner. As an African diaspora writer, Okorafor belongs to a new generation and her fiction represents a fresh voice in a genre that is dominated by male writers. The prolific nature of Nnedi Okorafor writings and the depth of her imagination as expressed in the majority of her Afrofuturist novels offer a new direction in African literature. Okorafor interrogates the postcolonial canon and breaks barriers to expand the frontiers of science fiction and magical realism.

Fantasy narratives and/or magical realism are genres that establish distinct parameters for interrogating the social, cultural, and political affairs of a people. While they tend to be far removed from a realistic portrayal of characters, settings, events and situations, they serve as a veritable source of mythic engagement with the culture of a particular people. The pervasive elements of the fictional universe of magical realism or fantasy novels resemble a mythological universe in which the writer attempts to understand the underlying philosophy behind the creation of myths. Christopher Warnes (2009) in *Magical Realism and the Postcolonial Novel* provides a basic definition of magical realism as "a mode of narration that naturalizes or normalises the supernatural; that is, a mode in which real and fantastic, natural, supernatural are coherently represented in a state of equivalence" (3). This equivalence shows magic as derived from the "supernatural" elements of "local" and indigenous religion, culture, and myths that speak directly to the historical, cultural, and literary aesthetics that are in all fictional texts. Myths may be defined as a "traditional story, typically involving supernatural beings or forces, which embodies and provides an explanation, aetiology or justification for something such as the early history of a society, a religious belief or ritual or a natural phenomenon" (OED). Myths are stories created from the human emotional adaptability and imaginations acted upon by her or his environment. The human origins, histories, legends, ancestors, and heroes become stories that shape a peoples' perspective and perceptions to their reality. Myths of origin stories reinforce how particular social orders are derived and propagated. Through these stories, there are justifications for certain patterns of behavior, gender roles, and male-female relationships in the society. Such stories thrive on the emotion and imaginations in response to the writer's surroundings. In creating a common meaning, and in order to challenge received models of social constructions, the writer relies on the shared imagination of the collective unconscious of the readers to defamiliarize the reality of these received notions. This has been the trend with many writers of magical realism including African writers employing mythical narratives in creative fictions.

Women writers, particularly African female writers through their works such as Buchi Emecheta's *Second Class Citizens* (1974), *Kehinde* (1994), Mariama Ba's *So Long a Letter* (1979), *Scarlet Song* (1981), Nawal El Saddawi's *Walking through Fire* (2002), *A Daughter of Isis* (1999), Ama

Ata Aidoo's *Changes* (1991), among others use their creative fictions and critical writings to engage and challenge domestic portrayals of the feminine gender both in the African terrain and in the diaspora. In the same manner, contemporary African women writers in such works as Tsitsi Dangaremba's *Nervous Conditions* (1988), *This Mournable Body* (2018), Chika Unigwe's *The Phoenix* (2007), *On Black Sisters' Street* (2007), Chimamanda Adichie's *Americanah* (2013), and Imbolo Mbue's *Behold the Dreamers* (2018) also take up the challenges of women writing in diasporic social settings. Their concerns usually range from issues in the family, community, and sociocultural problems that women face in the African society or in the diaspora. Consequently, their writings are primarily social-realist novels that portray the female as also capable of important roles in the society. They continue the tradition of engaging in feminist preoccupations with gender equality and overthrow of binary structures. In a sense, these writers as much as they focus on many issues that affect women, they rarely engage the magical realism form of the novel as an avenue to bring fresh perspectives to engage African mythologies. Rather, the male writers have tended to dominate this genre again, showcasing how the male writers remain a dominant force in African mythic narratives. Due to the wide-ranging engagements of women writers with social issues that affect women, the contemporary African literary canon has expanded (and is presently dominated by women) to include many female writers whether they write of African or diasporic experiences.

It is against this background that Nnedi Okorafor's stunning imagination in the Afrofuturistic, magical realism, and fantasy narratives is a new voice and a novel approach by an African female writer to enter the stronghold of a male-dominated space in African fiction. However, this is also helped by her incorporating ideals from a Western perspective of myth and fantasy narratives, and Afrofuturism established in the works of Octavia Butler. By creating a blend of mythical and realistic narratives, Okorafor creates a hybrid form of narratives that straddle different societies. The prolificacy of Nnedi Okorafor, and the depth of her imagination is expressed in majority of her novels that thrive on fantasia as a result of her conflicting cultural experiences.

JOSEPH CAMPBELL'S "MONOMYTH" AND ARCHETYPAL MYTHIC STRUCTURE

The overlap between fantasy novels and the real world allows the writer (and its characters) to reflect on contemporary social realities without the conventional methods of other fictional works. Fantasy narratives comment on existing ideologies, create and shape their own ideologies, and develop a structure that circumvents established canons in literature and human reality. With reference to the feminine engagement with speculative fantasy, magical realism, and Afrofuturism, this chapter contends that Okorafor follows the pattern of Joseph Campbell's monomyth structure where the heroes must necessarily confront evil forces that are more powerful than them; however, with the aid of cosmic forces, they overcome obstacles. This time, however, Okorafor gives prominent representation to her female characters at the forefront of both social and cultural significant changes. Joseph Campbell's monomyth, or the hero's journey, is "the common template of a broad category of tales that involve a hero who embarks on an adventure, and in a decisive crisis wins a victory, and then comes home changed and transformed" (Campbell, 1968: 30). According to Campbell, "A hero ventures forth from the world of common day into a region of supernatural wonder; fabulous forces are there encountered, and a decisive victory is won; the hero comes back from this mysterious adventure with the power to bestow boons on his fellow man" (30).

The narrative archetype, as propounded by Campbell compels readers to examine in close detail the narrative strategy adopted by Okorafor in *Who Fears Death* (2010) and *What Sunny Saw in the Flames* (2011). These works trace the heroine's adventure through wonderlands where she gains knowledge about the power, politics, and structure of her society. The protagonist's journey is Campbell's all-embracing metaphor of the deep inner transformation that heroes in every time and place seem to share, a path that leads them through great moments of separation, descent, ordeal, and return to the ordinary world where they question received assumptions. Although the heroes in myths and fantasy narratives embark on a physical journey, the physical journey is as important as the emotional or psychological journey. A character's actions and decisions in response to the journey's stages can reveal the character's arc, or phases of growth that are experienced during the unfolding story. The reader's engagement with the story is thus a way to defamiliarize myths in order to understand the sociocultural situations on which they thrive. Through this journey, both the characters and the readers realize that what they think they know becomes strange.

The monomyth structure—Campbell's pattern of *"separation–initiation–return"*—is the principal story that creates meaning for the life, which the author expounds. In following the heroes' adventure, it is evident that heroes are a product of time and place. But sometimes they transcend time and space, thus providing a complex tapestry of histories, myths, landscapes, rituals, and economic realities. This monomyth structure is basically a tripartite ensemble where there is separation from a familiar world, initiation into the world of magic, and return to ordinary world with knowledge hitherto hidden. The nuclear unit of the monomyth is such that the hero is separated and drawn away from her immediate and familiar environment into an unknown and unfamiliar terrain. The initiation into a higher calling thus presents her with a purpose and mission in life. Here, the hero is also made to understand that she is bestowed with a unique power that makes her privileged to be given such an enormous task. Her sojourn and adventures in the magical world constitute the major part of the journey (both physical and psychological) into experience as she figures out the reasons for her magical powers. After undergoing the challenges and having conquered, the hero returns to the familiar world again to bestow the boon on her people (Campbell, 1968: 35–37).

The novel in its most pliable form enables female writers to challenge long-held notions about the feminine gender in male-authored texts of African magical realism. The presentation of fantasy heroines and heroes is also largely biased toward the female characters as male characters tend to take a more prominent role. In adopting the fantasy, magic-realism, science-fiction form, Okorafor chooses a form that is sufficiently pliable to grapple with the most pressing questions of modern society in an altered world. And as Siobhan Carroll contends, the setting of Okorafor's novels "is not one in which science and magic, or science fiction and fantasy, occupy separate spaces" (Siobhan, 2015: 19). The fictive world of magical realism/fantasy shows that impossibilities are possible, where conventions of natural laws are altered. The adopted myths reinforce the common idea that what is impossible in the real world is highly possible and probable in the histories, geographies, and cultures of the spiritual world.

Nnedi Okorafor's Novels: Speculative Fiction and Afrofuturism

Nnedi Okorafor is a Nigerian-American writer of speculative fiction based in the United States. Some of her novels include *Zahrah the Windseeker* (2005), *Lagoon* (2007), *What Sunny Saw in the Flames* (2011), *Binti* (2015), *Who Fears Death* (2010), *The Book of Phoenix* (2015), and *The Shadow Speaker* (2007). Okorafor's novels have been likened to Western's fantasy novels and prose fictions like George R.R Martin's mythical world in *A Game of Thrones* (1996), *The Song of Ice and Fire* (1996), *A Dance with Dragons* (2011), and the HBO television film series "The Game of Thrones" where dragons, wolves, and other magical creatures are predominant and interact with human characters. J.R.R Tolkien's (1955) *The Lord of the Rings* and *The Hobbits* (1937) among other fantasy narratives with settings in "Middle Earth" are reminiscent of magical worlds where magic and surreal adventure are commonplace. J.K Rowling's (1997–2007) *Harry Potter* series is also fantasy narrative that has shaped reader's experience of Western narratives in speculative fiction and magical realism. Through a rich stylistic blend of African and American techniques in speculative fiction, Okorafor relates the African experience in magical realism with Western notions of fantasy in *Who Fears Death* (2010) and *What Sunny Saw in the Flames* (2011) to great effect.

In many of her novels, *Who Fears Death*, for example, Okorafor uses a combination of Western fantasy, African mythological narrative structures, new cultures, and a new world of heroes and heroines in her engagement with the sociopolitical problems of contemporary times. Fantasy takes place in an altered and most times an entirely new (or future) world created from the author's imagination. Okorafor's style is a blend of myths and histories of a non-Western culture and African culture in order to establish its settings as capable of supporting the fantasy narratives. In other words, the novel shows how a non-Western setting can be adopted to convey a sense of the African myth, politics, and history. Joshua Burnett (2015) characterizes Okorafor's writings as "speculative novels [that] are set either in future versions of Africa or in imagined worlds with strong West African cultural influences, and she takes a strongly postcolonial and feminist view within her fiction, at once championing African cultures and critiquing their gender roles and certain other cultural practices" (135).

Recently, the Marvel comic film "The Black Panther" (2018) is attributed to an Afrofuturistic portrayal of Africa and the world that is observable in Okorafor's novel. The fictive world of "Wakanda" in "The Black Panther" is similar to the world of the "Jhawir," "Okekes," and "Nurus" in *Who Fears Death*. Okorafor creates a time and space shift for her characters as they engage ordinary and mythical figures in political and cultural engagements. Okorafor blends the physical world (realism) and the supernatural world in a seamless transition. Her engagement with the mythical and surreal favorably compares with science fiction (sci-fi) fantasies of the American fictions, mirroring Butler's post-apocalyptic collapse of time in *Kindred*, for example. By blending two culturally different narratives (of myth), she shatters a male-dominated genre (especially in the African sense) in using her novels as a critique of the African and/or Western societies of patriarchal values encoded in some of these fantasy texts. In Okorafor's narratives, as *What Sunny Saw in the Flames* and *Who Fears Death* will make apparent in the subsequent paragraphs, the fusion of American and African mythical stories reinforces the stages of the hero's journey—physical and psychological. A journey (or movement) from the ordinary world (of ignorance, powerlessness, and fear) is quickly replaced by the supernatural (spiritual, magic, power, and fantasy) world in which everything is possible, thereby situating Nnedi Okorafor's novels in the speculative fiction and Afrofuturism genre.

The Hero's Adventure: Monomyth in
What Sunny Saw in the Flames

Joseph Campbell's monomyth of the character arc enables readers to examine the adventures of Sunny Nwanzue in *What Sunny Saw in the Flames* (first published as *Akata Witch*, 2010) as she struggles to reconcile the reality of her physical world and the surreal world of magic. The novel recreates the narrative strategy that Campbell finds common to all myths. In *What Sunny Saw in the Flames,* an evil creature, Black Hat Otokoto, powerful but twisted is on the rampage, abducting young and innocent children. The people are terrified, afraid to see the darkness, afraid to venture beyond their immediate environments. Amidst this general sense of insecurity, Sunny discovers that she can see into the future by looking at the flames. Born in New York, but living in Aba, Nigeria, 13-year-old Sunny is understandably a little lost. She is albino. Her eyes are so sensitive to the sun that she has to wait until evening to play football. Sunny feels estranged and an outcast in her family, among her peers in school, and in the community. Despite her natural abilities at soccer, she is not allowed to compete because of her gender, her albinism, and her limiting social conditions:

> My name is Sunny Nkeiruka Nwazue and I confuse people. I have two older brothers. Like my parents, my brothers were both born in Nigeria. . . . My parents felt it would be a better place to raise my brothers and me. They wanted us to know who we were and where we came from—at least that's what my mom says. . . . Being albino made the sun my enemy; my skin burned so easily that I felt nearly flammable. That's why, though I was really good at soccer, I couldn't join the boys when they played after school. They wouldn't let me anyway, me being a girl. (2)

From the beginning of the novel, her mixed heritage, identity, albinism, and gender already create a lacuna for where she could possibly find a sense of belonging in the family and in the society. Ethnic considerations of where she was born, who her parents are, and where she lives make her an outcast in the "ordinary" human world. Sunny's place in the family is quite unlike that of her brothers. She does not find any affinity with her father as a result of her albinism and powers, neither is her mother effective in helping her understand the deep connection she shared with her grandmother. She says of the ordinary human world in which she lives:

> Sometimes I hated my father, sometimes I felt he hated me, too. I couldn't help that I wasn't the son he wanted or the pretty daughter he'd accepted instead. But I couldn't not see what I saw in that candle. And I couldn't help what I eventually became. (3)

Because Sunny is out of place in the human world, she is drawn closer to Orlu, Chichi, and Sasha. Once she becomes aware of what she is, it becomes ultimately difficult to reconcile the indeterminable gulf between the ordinary world she has grown accustomed to and the alluring but frightening world of the "Leopard" people that beckons to her. It is established that being one of the Leopard people is never coincidental. Rather it speaks of a lineage from which someone must trace their ancestry. Sunny's progenitor is clouded with secrecy that she must find the answers for herself through a magic box left for her by her grandmother, which guides her. As the friendship and cultural/ancestral/historical exchanges among the young heroes—Sunny, Orlu, Chichi, and Sasha—begin to take concrete shape, they are drawn into the covert world of the Leopard people through magic and witchcraft.

Sunny, Orlu, Chichi, and Sasha's emergence at the time they are just discovering their magical abilities is not unconnected to their seeming out of sort with the ordinary human world, whereas they find acceptance in a magical world or cult of powerful magic. In this world, every inhibition is removed and their beauty, power and complementary strengths become a trademark and hallmark for a compelling adventure narrative. In this fantastical world, they are schooled on the history of their powers, their heritage, how others before them have tried and failed to overcome Black Hat Otokoto, and how evil always seem to overcome even the strongest who have been "chosen" to confront it. However, because the hero's journey is what is driving the story, we are encouraged in the knowledge that they will succeed, even at great perils to their magical powers.

This monomyth therefore provides insight into the ways in which Okorafor uses her hero's journey to reflect both the structural and cultural patterns that define Afrofuturism. In the landscape(s) of the novel, the characters have hierarchy, order, master-servant/apprentice relationship depending on gifts and temperament. They engage in trade, religion, sports, and politics. An existing problem surfaces at about the time the heroes are just discovering their true powers and purpose. A problem arises and a call to take up a role is bestowed on the hero as she navigates the weight of confronting and solving the problems posed. The hero must then enter the spiritual world as a novice but with the aid of helpers and allies of complementary powers defeat the enemy and restore balance to the world. Chichi, Orlu, and Sasha act as complementary figures to Sunny in this quest set before her. At first, it seems everyone but Sunny understands who they are and the powers they possess. Their different abilities and powers they soon realize are complementary for the cause they have been chosen to undertake. For instance, Orlu can reverse any kind of magic, while Chichi can remember everything she reads or summon any spirit to fight her enemies. Sunny herself, though a free agent, is endowed with shape-shift abilities. Even as the task seems impossible, the readers' understanding of the ordinary world allows us to identify with the characters. We identify with the heroes' drives, urges, and problems while showing unique characteristics and flaws that make them three dimensional. Without the risks and dangers of the likelihood of failure, the audience will not be compelled to be a part of the heroes' journey.

As the narration of the novel straddles between realism and the magical, the fantasy world of *What Sunny Saw in the Flames* shows that it is not only magical but also presents the economics, educational model, medicine ("Juju"), and political structure of the Leopard people and their society. Sunny has to be initiated into this way of life that thrives on the mastery of magical powers. However, she must take her time to understand the dynamics and the true extent of her powers. Her initiation then gives her every purpose to which her gift can be tailored. In achieving her goal, Sunny is rarely alone but is aided by allies, mentors, and friends of like or complementary powers in her confrontation with the enemy. The description of Black Hat Otokoto as the villain reinforces the adventure story in most mythologies where the hero has to confront a more powerful force. Black Hat Otokoto has all but attained the highest level of the mastery of magic. Therefore, he is as powerful as all the other mentors and leadership structures the children encounter. He becomes a real threat because the heroes cannot individually face him and hope to win. The complementary nature of their powers ensures that they develop human virtues of love, courage, and sacrifice in their struggles, with Sunny a female character at the forefront of defeating Black Hat Otokoto. These attributes endear the reader to the heroes as they proceed precariously in their one quest to overcome the enemy. The awareness of the impending battles imbues them with the drive to overcome all adversaries. The spiritual world contrasts with the ordinary world they are coming from and as they become more conscious of their roles, they develop the desire to succeed against all odds and to right any perceived wrong. At the end, through combined efforts, they defeat Black Hat Otokoto and restore balance to both the ordinary world and the supernatural world.

The Hero's Confrontation: Monomyth in *Who Fears Death*

Who Fears Death (2010) tells the story of the people of a Seven River Kingdom, particularly of the two warring factions, the Nurus and the Okekes, who have a deep-rooted hatred for each other. The war is predominantly genocidal, for the purpose of domination and subjugation. It is a war of superiority and enslavement. These elements have existed for ages until the major character, Onyesonwu is born amidst the brutality of war, rape, and violence that characterize the age-long rivalry between the ethnic communities. The more powerful Nuru people rape and maim the weak Okeke such that any child conceived of such brutality is marked as an outcast (*Ewu*) to both the Nurus and the Okekes. Onyesonwu's story, as the protagonist, is a personal quest for liberation of herself and her people. It begins with ignorance of her history, of her mother's past, and her biological father. She is born far removed from the epic theatre of a war that drives her mother far into the desert until she settles in a community of Jhawir, where *Ewu* children are despised for their impure blood. Onyesonwu finds out early enough that she is clearly an outcast because of the isolated life she lives with her mother in the desert. She also understands that she and her mother do not belong in the community where they reside. The resentment from everyone means that as she grew, she confronts many obstacles to full acceptance in a community either steeped in ignorance or rigidly structured to exempt her from its magical/spiritual world. However, she is able to manipulate magic intuitively. She later finds out that possessing magical abilities is not a curse rather it is a rare gift that allows her to fight for her people and re-write their "myth" and history. As Onyesonwu comes to terms with her magical abilities when her adopted father dies; she realizes that she has a more important quest to liberate the Okeke people from enslavement and bring about the needed revolution to set the warring factions on a new course.

Onyesonwu's birth is brutal. Her mother's experience in the hands of the powerful sorcerer, Daib, and through the many years in the wilderness allows readers to understand the circumstances that Campbell establishes as fabulous in the conception of the hero; that is, separation from the familiar and ordinary human world, initiation into the world of magic and witchcraft/sorcery, descent or crossing into the threshold, numerous ordeals in the hands of more powerful adversaries, conquest, and finally, a return to the ordinary world with knowledge (or in the case of Onyesonwu, liberation of her people).

Onyesonwu's powers, derived from her mother's telekinetic abilities and her sorcerer father, establishes her pedigree (first as an outcast tainted with "impure" blood (*Ewu*) and then a female in a rigidly patriarchal structure of both the human world and the supernatural world of the Okekes) to undertake the task of fighting for the oppressed and marginalized, thus creating a monomyth for her adventure. However, because of her gender, acceptance into the world of magic becomes harder than she thought when she finds it most difficult to find a more powerful sorcerer to train her to channel these magical powers.

The assumptions in the magical world of Okorafor's *Who Fears Death* are given. Only male sorcerers are capable of important roles. Women are subaltern and are not allowed the mystic mysteries of the hallowed grounds in which magic reign supreme. Readers are asked to follow the struggles of this female character as she navigates the rigid structures that deny her agency and the series of tests (magical, mental, and physical), which she has to undergo in order to prove her worthiness to practice magic. She is constantly reminded of her limits as she prepares for the great "battle" with Daib—a battle that has personal significance for liberating her people.

Onyesonwu is gifted with the combined powers of time and space travel, healing, magic, and shape-shifting into any animal. Her powers nonetheless, combined with her mentor's grueling training, after many rejections because she is a woman, ensure she is able to control the Mystic Points in the fantasy world of the narrative, a feat thought impossible because she is female. In her training, Aro, her mentor and teacher, observes that Onyesonwu possesses the natural abilities already to work the Mystic Points in her quest to confront the powerful sorcerer Daib but fears that because she is woman she cannot get to the highest level of control:

> The Mystic Points are aspects of everything. A sorcerer can manipulate them with his tools to make things happen. It's not the "magic" of children's stories. To work the Points is far beyond any juju. "There are four points," he said loudly. "Okike, Alusi, Mmuo, Uwa." ". . . The Uwa Point represents the physical world, the body," Aro said. "Change, death, life, connection. You're Eshu. That is your tool to manipulate it with." "The Mmuo Point is the wilderness," the Alusi point represents forces, deities, spirits, non-Uwa beings. Lastly, the Okike Point represents the Creator. This point cannot be touched. No tool can turn the back of the Creator toward what It has created. (139)

The Mystic Points are directional powers that helped Onyesonwu to overcome her greatest enemy. In the hero's quest, she is supported by friends and allies who travel with her across the seven kingdoms on her liberatory quest. Mwita is a character that acts as the alter ego to Onyesonwu in the narrative. In a way, Okorafor transposes the traditional roles of both sexes as Onyesonwu has the masculine powers of sorcery and Mwita, the healer who has usually feminine roles in fantasy. Nonetheless, Mwita, as the healer rather than the sorcerer, helps her to maintain balance and control of her emotions, which sometimes threaten to overthrow the balance of the narrative. Having accomplices helped Onyesonwu achieve a greater sense of purpose and clarity as to the import of her adventure. Onyesonwu, as the participant narrator gives the adventure some semblance of intimacy, as she brings the readers into both the physical and spiritual worlds of the Nurus and Okekes.

Okorafor's narrative in *Who Fears Death* confronts issues such as female genital cutting, war, and genocide while also challenging existing norms and traditions that create gender inequality. Onyesonwu faces social perceptions that deny her essence as a human being. She faces opposition because first she's an outcast, born of rape. And secondly, because she is a female, her biological father's hatred for her is because she is not who he wants her to be (that is, a male child). Aro, who eventually becomes her trainer and mentor, will not teach her at first because of her gender until she proves her skill in manipulating magic. Given extraordinary powers in the invented mythical world of the novel, Onyesonwu becomes more important in the concerns of the author to engage with contemporary issues confronting the female gender in African societies.

By allowing readers to see the narrative through Onyesonwu's perspective, readers are drawn into her battles against powerful forces of a predominantly patriarchal society where the outcasts are regarded as prostitute or useless: "In Jhawir, Ewu people were outcast. In Banza, Ewu women were prostitutes. It was no good wherever I went" (192). As she traverses the physical and supernatural worlds, her powers grow, her ability for self-control increases, and her senses heighten and she is able to liberate all the women by obliterating all the males in Nuru, making all the women pregnant at the same time, thereby establishing the narrative for re-writing a new history and a new order. In a similar circumstance to *What Sunny saw in the Flame*, the ultimate villain in *Who Fears Death*, Daib, grows complacent and underestimates the element of surprise that the hero comes up with simply because she's a female. The sheer willpower and the overriding fortune that goes with heroes in these mythic patterns are evidently abounded to make them victorious—a structure Okorafor clearly manipulates to show her female protagonists as capable of achieving lasting victories. Therefore, what we see and understand through the characters of Sunny and Onyesonwu, Okorafor, according to Mariam Pahl, "lays the great weight on the future, its anticipation and (on her own) responsibility to actively shape it" (220). Through this effort, a new voice is heralded in the discussion of women actively engaged in magical realism as a novel form.

CONCLUSION

This chapter explores Nnedi Okorafor's fantasy narratives through the monomyth pattern set by Joseph Campbell in exploring the life of her major characters Sunny and Onyesonwu in *What Sunny Saw in the Flames* and *Who Fears Death*, respectively. Campbell presents a monomyth pattern that universally represents different cultures of myth around the world. Through this patterning, we identify the hero's physical and psychological journey, a journey that represents the pattern of human life and growth within the defined experience. Both Sunny and Onyesonwu find themselves as outcasts as well as outside of the structure that limits their capacity for sustained revolution based on gender. Their triumph over many limiting paradigms serves as a way for Okorafor to break barriers and establish herself as an important voice in the

Afrofuturism genre. Within the broader perspectives of feminism, Okorafor engages with the structural pattern of Afrofuturism to present her characters, particularly the female heroes, as capable of questioning received ideas that inhibit them. They thus become the vehicle through which Okorafor situates her novels within contemporary discussions around themes as male-female relationship, race, gender, and inequality. As the heroes move from a state of ignorance to experience, the readers are drawn into their worlds, both physical and spiritual, to relive their own fears and fantasy. Okorafor's writings thus emerge as a nodal point in women engaging actively in traditional and non-traditional narrative patterns to break barriers both in traditional genres and storytelling. Okorafor's feminine engagement with magical realism breaks into a genre that is largely skewed against women either as writer in the African context or their characters as they confront social and cultural inhibitions.

REFERENCES

Adichie, Chimamanda. 2013. *Americanah*. New York: Alfred A. Knopf.
Aidoo, Ama Ata. 1991. *Changes*. New York: The Feminist Press at CUNY.
Ba, Mariama. 1979. *So Long a Letter*. UK: Heinemann.
Ba, Mariama. 1981. *Scarlet Song*. London: Pearson.
Burnett, Joshua. 2015. "The Great Change and the Great Book: Nnedi Okorafor's Postcolonial, Post-Apocalyptic Africa and the Promise of Black Speculative Fiction." *Research in African Literatures, What Is Africa to Me Now?* 46(4): 133–150. https://www.jstor.org/stable/10.2979/reseafrilite.46.4.133.
Butler, Octavia. 1979. *Kindred*. Boston: Beacon Press.
Butler, Octavia. 1987. *Dawn*. New York: Grand Central Publishing.
Butler, Octavia. 1988. *Adulthood Rites*. New York: Grand Central Publishing.
Butler, Octavia. 1989. *Imago*. New York: Grand Central Publishing.
Butler, Octavia. 1993. *Parable of the Talent*. New York: Grand Central Publishing.
Butler, Octavia. 2012. *Parable of the Sower*. New York: Seven Stories Press.
Campbell, Joseph. 1968. *The Hero with the Thousand Faces*. 2nd edition. Boston: Princeton.
Carroll, Siobhan. 2015. "Nnedi Okorafor: An Introduction." *Journal of the Fantastic in the Arts* 26(1): 19–20. www.jstor.org/stable/26321076.
Coogler, Ryan. 2018. *Black Panther*. Marvel Cinema.
Dangarembga, Tsitsi. 1988. *Nervous Conditions*. California: Seal Press.
Dangarembga, Tsitsi. 2018. *This Mournable Body*. Minnesota: Graywolf Press.
Duiker, K. Sello. 2011. *The Hidden Star*. Cape Town, SA: Umuzi.
El Sadaawi, Nawal. 1999. *A Daughter of Isis*. London: Zed Books.
El Sadaawi, Nawal. 2002. *Walking Through Fire*. London: Zed Books.
Emecheta, Buchi. 1974. *Second Class Citizen*. New York: George Braziller Inc.
Emecheta, Buchi. 1994. *Kehinde*. UK: Heinemann.

Martin, George R. R. 1996a. *A Game of Thrones*. New York: Bantam.
Martin, George R. R. 1996b. *A Song of Fire and Ice*. New York: Bantam.
Martin, George R. R. 2011. *A Dance with Dragons*. UK: Harper Voyager.
Mbue, Imbolo. 2016. *Behold the Dreamers*. New York: Random House.
Okorafor, Nnedi. 2005. *Zahrah the Windseeker*. Houghton Miffin Co.
Okorafor, Nnedi. 2007a. *Lagoon*. UK: Hodder & Stoughton.
Okorafor, Nnedi. 2007b. *The Shadow Speaker*. New York: Disney Book/Hyperion.
Okorafor, Nnedi. 2010. *Who Fears Death*. New York: Daw Books.
Okorafor, Nnedi. 2011. *What Sunny Saw in the Flames*. Abuja: Cassava Republics.
Okorafor, Nnedi. 2015a. *Binti*. Tor.com.
Okorafor, Nnedi. 2015b. *The Book of Phoenix*. New York: Daw Books.
Okri, Ben. 1991. *The Famished Road*. New York: Anchor Books.
Pahl, Miriam. 2018. "Time, Progress, and Multidirectionality in Nnedi Okorafor's *Who Fears Death*." *Research in African Literature* 49(3): 207–222. http://www.jstor.org/stable/10.2979/reseafrilite.49.3.12.
Ratterman, Debra. 1991. "Octavia Butler: Writer." *Off Our Back* 21(5): 26–27. http://www.jstor.org/stable/200833592.
Rowlings, Joanne. 1997–2007. *Harry Potter*. New York: Scholastic Inc.
Tolkien, J. 1937. *The Hobbits*. Boston: Houghton Miffin Harcourt.
Tolkien, J. R. R. 1955. *The Lord of the Rings*. Boston: Houghton Miffin Harcourt.
Unigwe, Chika. 2007. *The Phoenix*. Lagos: Farafina.
Vogler, Christopher. 1999. "Excerpts from Myths and the Movies, Stuart Voytilla" (n.d.) in Stuart Voytilla, *Myth and the Movies: Discovering the Mythic Structure of 50 Unforgettable Films*. Michael Wiese Productions.
Warnes, Christopher. 2009. *Magical Realism and the Postcolonial Novel*. UK: Palgrave Macmillan.
Wa Thiong'o, Ngugi. 2008. *Wizard of the Crow*. New York: Pantheon.

Conclusion

Shifting the Boundaries of African Women's Writing

Rose A. Sackeyfio

African Women Writing Diaspora: Transnational Perspectives in the 21st Century engages the fluid and shifting boundaries of African women's lives in the global age. For African emigres, the globalized world marks a new reality of intersecting borders, changing landscapes, and bifurcated identities within multilocal spaces beyond the African continent. New developments in the contemporary African novel may be conceptualized as growing pains that shift the boundaries of an evolving aesthetic of literary production. The transcontinental gaze of female authors who live between worlds as diaspora subjects has actualized literary transitions and multilayered themes that span postcolonial, postmodern, and contemporary landscapes.

Driven by global movement of people, commodities, and ideas and the transformative energies of social, economic, and political upheaval, African migration channels creative artistry of a new literary generation that is led by women. Carol Boyce Davies in *Black Women Writing and Identity* (1994) posits: "The re-negotiating of identities is fundamental to migration as it is fundamental to black women's writing in cross-cultural contexts. It is the convergence of multiple places and cultures that re-negotiates the terms of black women's experience that in turn negotiates and re-negotiate their identities (3). The volume interprets the ways in which contemporary fictional works interrogate the complexities of new identities and new ways of being African in the world.

Critical approaches to contemporary African literature include a reflection on Afropolitan lifestyles and aesthetics in the experiences of authors that parallel the transnational characters in their fictional works. The novels that are explored in the collection engage diverse narratives of difference, marginality, and identity that subvert essentialist claims of *Afropolitan* identity for African diaspora subjects. Some of the works examined in the collection are partially autobiographical through the lived experiences as transnational subjects in America and Europe.

Taiye Selasie's controversial essay "Bye Bye Babar" (2005) launched a popular but widely debated term to describe a new brand of globetrotting African immigrants who live *Afropolitan* lifestyles that are projected in glowing and elated terms. Selasie's essay may be read as a celebration of successful immigrants who are:

> African young people working and living in cities around the globe, they belong to no single geography, but feel at home in many. They, (read we) are Afropolitans—the newest generation of African emigrants, coming soon or collected already at a law firm/chem lab/jazz lounge near you.... You'll know us by our funny blend of London fashion, New York jargon, African ethnic mixes, Ghanaian and Canadian, Nigerian and Swiss.... We are Afropolitans, ... not citizens but Africans of the world. (Selasie, 2005: 5)

Selasie's life is indeed *Afropolitan* through her mobility, family background, and cultural hybridity because she was born in London to Nigerian, Ghanaian, and Scottish parents, raised in Boston and studied in Yale and Oxford. She has lived in New Delhi, Accra, Rome, and Berlin. Her life captures the savvy, cosmopolitan flavor of a class dynamic that she generalizes in ways that suggest a new kind of "single story" for African people in foreign spaces.

The term has become part of the discourse that engages the fluid and shifting identities of characters in much of contemporary immigrant fiction. With the exception of Yaa Gyasi's *Homegoing* and Okorafor's futuristic settings in *Who Fears Death* and *What Sunny Saw in the Flames*, Sefi Atta, Chimamanda Ngozi Adiche, and No Violet Bulawayo's works express Afropolitan elements. Calixthe Beyala and Fatima Diallo's novels are works of Francophone fiction that vividly describe immigrant life in France, but in all of the works, the female gaze belies the harsh realities of racial inequality, the difficulties of legal status, and economic adversity among other challenges to happiness.

Broadly speaking, Afropolitanism can be defined as "cosmopolitanism with African roots" according to Gehrmann (2016: 61), but the term conveys perceptions that are reductionist, and narcissistic and suggest a single-storied reality derived from elitism born of socioeconomic status and privilege. Simon Gikandi, largely supports the salient features of *Afropolitanism* in the foreword to *Negotiating Afropolitanism: Essays on Borders and Spaces in Contemporary Literature and Folklore* (2011). However, he acknowledges the "negative consequences of transnationalism, the displacement of Africans abroad, the difficulties they face as they try to overcome their alterity in alien landscapes, and the deep cultural anxieties that often make diasporas sites of cultural fundamentalism and ethnic chauvinism" (11). The women characters in the fictional works discussed in *African Women Writing Diaspora* represent vivid and compelling portraits of the downside of immigrant life through the lens of gender.

The range of experiences of female protagonists explored in the collection is diverse, and sadly, the sex workers in Unigwe's *On Black Sisters' Street* and Amma Darko's *Beyond the Horizon* embody the worst elements of transnational identity for African women. Cheryl Toman's chapter on "Malian Immigrants in France" and Amanda Laji's "Waithood and Girlhood," as well as Sackeyfio's analysis of *News from Home* by Sefi Atta exemplify the challenges of diaspora life in France and America, respectively. Finally, Adichie's Ifemelu, Atta's Deola, and Ama Ata Aidoo's Sissie are transnational subjects plagued by racial otherness and marginality that unravel Gikandi's framing of "negative consequences of transnationalism" discussed above.

The more positive insights of Afropolitan framing are its merit to counter prevailing monolithic and stereotypical representations of the "abject African immigrant" across Europe and America. This class of African migrants may be perceived as largely undocumented, likely fleeing conflict as a refugee, and generally unskilled, existing on the margins of society, while struggling against a web of barriers to equality, employment, and legal status in foreign nations hostile to their presence. Selasie's coinage of *Afropolitan* identities is actually a timely and cogent re-framing of translocal Africans who may contribute to multiple urban locales in the form of education, creativity, and specialized skills. Gikandi notes, "Fitting neatly into traditional Western notions of Africa as the 'other' of modern reason and progress, Afropessimism has proven hard to dislodge because it seems to be the only logical response to political failure and economic stagnation in Africa" (2011: 9).

The negative perceptions of Africans have more to do with the dynamics of race, colonial legacies, and the complexities of social, economic, and political trends within industrialized nations of the West than the threat of nations being destabilized by unwelcome African populations. Taiye Selasie's intervention asserts African agency, success, and the formation of credential carrying migrants as a new brand of transnational subjects in the global environment of the twenty-first century.

While the description above is oppositional to Afropessimistic sentiments of African and non-African critique, it is essentialist in nature and thoroughly misleading through the exclusion of other populations of Africans who are less fortunate in acquiring education, mobility, and the trappings of material comfort outside the continent. Unigwe's *On Black Sisters' Street* and Amma Darko's *Beyond the Horizon* fall into this category as well as Akachi Adimora's *Trafficked* (2008).

A host of scholars, and critics of African literature, as well as contemporary writers have rejected or modified the use of Afropolitanism altogether.

In "Bye Bye Babar," Selasie raises questions of image and representation of *all* Africans that navigate multiple spaces in the world. Author and social critic Emma Dabiri affirms: "We are now well versed in the danger of a single story. While *Afropolitanism* may appear to offer an alternative to the single story, we run the danger of this becoming the dominant narrative for African success" (2014: 6). There is no real danger in the above scenario for the simple reason that regardless of education, or socioeconomic status, racial dynamics permeate the lives of people of color worldwide. Systemic racism and other forms of inequality drive the social, economic, and political outcomes of Africans and African descended peoples throughout the world whether they are citizens of a developed nation or not.

More importantly, the contemporary African novel categorically explores diaspora themes as an evolving aesthetic in the genre. In addition to Gyasi's debut with the publication of *Homegoing*, Imbolo Mbue's *Behold the Dreamers* (2016) and Nana Offoriata Ayim's *The God Child* (2019) compliment an array of fiction that traverse diaspora settings. Somali Italian writer, Igiaba Scego published *Adua* in 2015, and Bernadine Evaristo won the 2019 Man Booker Prize for an astounding collection of short stories titled *Girl, Woman, Other*, whose characters chronicle the lives of black British women. Finally, The airplane on the cover of Chika Unigwe's new collection of short fiction commands readers' attention to mobility and the transnational encounter for African immigrants in Belgium. Published in 2019, the collection is aptly called *Better Never than Late* as a vivid rendering of "stories about the tragedy of arrival and the yearning for home." Most of the titles of these new works gesture to the tensions, contradictions, and challenges that African migrants experience.

The overwhelming focus on diaspora themes in this body of works is quite literally a sign of the times as a marker of transformation and global movement to new frontiers of shifting identities for African immigrants.

The problem with *Afropolitanism* is not that it is wholly inaccurate, but that it is conceptualized from a vantage point of elitism and socioeconomic privilege and presented through a self-congratulatory effluence that generalizes all African migrants. Moreover, Nigerian scholar and critic, Chielozona Eze, affirms: "the more damning weakness of the term . . . is in its exclusivity and elitism." Adichie's Ifemelu and Atta's Deola are more representative of Afropolitan characters than other female protagonists in the novels examined. Their education affords them the benefit of travel, which sharpens their gaze outward in ways that contextualize their subalterity in the West. Henaku's analysis teases out the modalities of what she calls the "oppositional gaze."

The chapter "Transnational African Women as voices of Conscience: Aidoo's *Our Sister Killjoy*, Adichie's *Americanah* and Atta's *A Bit of Difference*" unravels Ifemelu's sojourn in America to interpret a richly textured account of an African woman using her agency and intellect to rediscover herself, along with her potential to "speak back and across borders." Through Ifemelu's blog, her positionality forges the deconstruction of racial hierarchies and the legacy of racial oppression in America, hybridity, otherness, and misrepresentation of African women. In *Americanah*, Ifemelu, after 13 years in America, eventually comes full circle as a sophisticated professional whose gaze eventually turns homeward to Nigeria.

With reference to Atta's *A Bit of Difference*, Henaku points out that Deola, the protagonist, is employed with an international charity organization where she experiences the hegemonic structures of global humanitarian work and racial otherness. Deola's education, travel to distant places like America and India, and exposure to other viewpoints are in and of themselves Afropolitan in nature and at the same time a route to becoming a "voice of conscience," awakened feminist impulse, and renewed connection to Nigeria as her homeland.

Ama Ata Aidoo's *Our Sister Killjoy* or *Reflections of a Black Eyed Squint* is an iconic work of postcolonial fiction that foregrounds literary engagement with diaspora themes along with Emecheta's *In The Ditch* (1972), *Second Class Citizen* (1974), and *Kehinde* (1994) that are set in London. Sissie's experiences in Germany motivate the "oppositional consciousness" in relation to the colonial collision, her relationship with a German woman, the abrasive encounters as a racial "other," and the perceptions of her fellow African students. She is unsophisticated as opposed to contemporary African women characters like Ifemelu or Deola, but her eyes are open and she "gets it." Like all the women in the novels examined, she too becomes a "voice of conscience" through reimagining her identity in Germany. Henaku notes that Sissie returns the gaze, and in the act of seeing herself through the eyes of others her Ghanaian identity she is grounded or perhaps reinforced by the racialized encounters in Germany. Similar to Ifemelu and Deola, she returns home to Ghana. Although several decades separate the works, the similarities of racial difference and marginalization link the works through the voices of women who narrate their subjectivity.

Simon Gikandi offers a nuanced interpretation of an Afropolitanism that:

> has been prompted by the desire to think of African identities as both rooted in specific local geographies but also transcendent of them. To be Afropolitan is to be connected to knowable African communities, languages and states. It is to embrace and celebrate a state of cultural hybridity - to be of African and other worlds at the same time. (2011: 9)

Gikandi's articulation is a reasoned, logical elucidation of Afropolitanism that succeeds in contextualizing its use in the global African imaginary. His iteration accommodates a more nuanced reading of the term that through literary criticism may enhance our understanding of the complexities of African migrant life as portrayed in fictional works.

In response to the commodification and implicit orientation toward consumerism, Wachira Kigotho in "Pan-African versus Afropolitans-An Identity Crisis?" notes Bingavanga Wainina's response to Afropolitanism "as a crude and cultural product, designed and potentially funded by the west." "I am a Pan-Africanist, not an Afropolitan" (2). Stated in no uncertain terms, Wainina's rejection of the term is echoed by Chimamanda Ngozi Adichie in an interview where she "counters Afropolitanism succinctly: 'I'm not Afropolitan. I'm African, happily so . . . I'm comfortable in the world, and it's not that unusual.' Many Africans are happily African and don't think they need a new term." Like Deola, Ifemelu's inner journeys in *Americanah* lead her happily back to Nigeria as the novel ends on a note of acceptance of herself as an African, and unapologetically Igbo.

Tomi Adeaga highlights the vulnerability of African women in the international sex trade through interrogation of trafficked women characters in Unigwe's *On Black Sisters Street* and Amma Darko's *Beyond the Horizon.* In juxtaposing the two works, Adeaga highlights the intertextual elements and interlocking forces of women's oppression. Patriarchy, poverty, and sexual exploitation cause vulnerable females to be lured and entrapped in a form of modern-day slavery.

In "Black Women's Bodies in a Global Economy: Sex, Lies and Slavery," Sackeyfio draws attention to sexual commodification of African women as part of the dark underbelly of globalization and notes that:

> Chika Unigwe has skillfully illustrated commonalities among the individual stories of the women because they are all exploited by males who not only denigrate them but place them at risk for violence and tragedy. Dele is cast as a wealthy and shrewd individual whose involvement in the sex trade underscores how unequal gender relations and patriarchal values underlie the entrapment of women in the sex trade industry. Trafficking women for economic exploitation is a predictable outcome of development challenges such as poverty, population displacement by internal conflicts and lack education and opportunities and opportunities for females. (205)

Both novels display the complexities of women's subjectivity through the sexual objectification of the black female body.

The meaning of diaspora, in all its variegated forms and expressions frames the intertextual representations of women's lives in the works examined in the collection. *African Women Writing Diaspora* looks at new ways of telling the African story through the female gaze from multicontinental settings. Nana Wilson-Tagoe in "The African Novel and the Feminine Condition" notes that

> To explore the feminine condition in the African novel is to examine how these wider ramifications of women's lives are mapped, interrogated and reinvented in the medium of the novel. The novel's capacity to map and reorganize reality has made it the most convenient medium for African writers seeking to rethink their social worlds in transitional and postcolonial times. (177)

As a broadly sketched work of historical fiction, Gyasi's *Homegoing* is an epic rendering of the transition to African diaspora identity, through the trauma of the Atlantic Slave trade, plantation life in Alabama, and generational linkages to Ghana. Unlike the other works in the collection, memory and symbolism of cultural moorings lay the groundwork for wholesome remembrance and reconnection to the African past in Ghana. Gyasi's artistry has woven a tapestry of the lineage history of two half-sisters that began in seventeenth-century Ghana. A salient feature, and perhaps the major strength of the work, is the connecting threads of family ties to the protagonist in the twenty-first century in America.

In *Homegoing*, renewed cultural linkages resonate through historical events in Ghana as a site of trauma and cleavage during slavery that resulted in the creation of the African diaspora in the Americas. Thus, memory of Africa in the novel functions very differently from the other works in the volume because the female protagonist who dominates the latter chapters of the novel has never lived in Ghana and grew up in Alabama in United States. The recollections of several ancestral figures represent collective identity and are motifs that take on a life of their own through the complex chronological structure of the work. Moreover, the African diaspora characters represent the descendants of the first migration of Africans who were captured during the Atlantic Slave Trade as opposed to voluntary migration in the twentieth and twenty-first centuries. *Homegoing* succeeds as a work of diaspora or immigrant fiction because through the lens of history notions of what it means to be African, and the question of return to one's ancestral homeland are explored in ways that impart lessons for Africans and African descended people in the global age.

Sackeyfio's chapter on Sefi Atta's *News from Home* illuminates the awakened consciousness of a young Nigerian woman whose diaspora journey is fraught with uncertainty. Her experiences are juxtaposed alongside the rising activism among women in her hometown in the Niger Delta. Atta's novella sharpens the transnational gaze from abroad to shed light on women's response to environmental degradation, severe poverty, and desperation in the oil-rich region of southeastern Nigeria. Although she has a nursing degree, unemployment back home has left her with few choices to survive. Atta connects postcolonial themes to interrogate Nigeria's failure to achieve the promise of independence and rescue their citizens from economic malaise and political corruption. Eve, the protagonist, is similar to female characters in her novel *Swallow* (2008). In this work, young Nigerian women are trapped in poverty with limited opportunities for success and happiness. The decades-long neglect, environmental devastation, and the attendant diseases, birth defects, political violence, and impoverishment blur the future of young women like Eve.

Eve is not an Afropolitan because of her undocumented status and she works as a nanny in New Jersey. The diaspora setting becomes a site of agency as she plans her future in America. Unlike Deola, in Atta's *A Bit of Difference*, the option to return home to Nigeria is untenable. This suggests the author's message that many young people have a bleak future in Africa because of unfavorable realities and lack of opportunities for upward mobility, even when they are educated.

Speculative Fiction opens a space for innovation in the creation of new identities within imagined futures for African subjects. Through Magical Realism, and Afrofuturist elements, Nnedi Okorfaor's *Who Fears Death* and *What Sunny Saw in the Flames* display the potential for women's empowerment and agency to navigate their destinies.

Sackeyfio's "Female Power, Transformation and Re-imagined Futures in Nnedi Okorafor's *Lagoon*" notes that "this body of works conveys the ways in which speculative fiction by black women has shifted the boundaries of imaginary landscapes to foreground the vitality of female power(s) in shaping the future (1). Okorafor's fantastical young women use their powers to effect change and to right the wrongs imposed by society such as gender inequality, outcasting, violence, and other forms of oppression in societies that are set in imaginary landscapes. The females in both works come of age in ways that challenge norms and expectations within rigid and patriarchal spaces.

Coming of age shapes NoViolet Bulawyo's *We Need New Names* as it engages the concept of "waithood" for the displaced protagonist Darling, who migrates from deeply troubled Zimbabwe to *Destroyed Michigan*. Like the other diasporic women in the accompanying fictional works, her new life is torn by conflict and ruptured existence between two worlds of difference in Africa and America. Her memories of Zimbabwe recall the desperate poverty of her childhood, life as a street child in Harare, and the splintered family she left behind.

Amanda Lagji illustrates the complexities of suspension and liminality that are evident at the end of the novel when, years later, Darling's identity and connection to her homeland are sharply challenged by her childhood friend. One might observe that the novel is more of a journey into confusion than a transition to adulthood. Helon Habila's critique of *We Need New Names* as "poverty porn" is questionable and contradictory in view of the freedom of writer's to "write what they know," expressed by James Baldwin (2013: qtd. in "Things Come Together" 45). Mukoma Wa Ngugi says of Bulawayo that she is "writing from what she knows, and in her times. She raises issues that are outside the radar of the traditional African novel" (2013: 45). Moreover, Bulawayo is among the generation of African writers who are actively shifting the boundaries of literature as a mirror of new challenges, themes, and experiences in the global age.

Francophone African literature is also expanding the boundaries of women's writing and Calixthe Beyala's *Loukoum: The "Little Prince" of Belleville* (1992) and Fatimata Diallo's *Sous mon voile* "Under my veil" (2015). The two works are written 23 years apart, the intertextual elements of the text uncover the history of Malian immigration in France. Both works express strong feminist ideas and Diallo's account is autobiographical. Cheryl Toman explicates the intimate portraits of female subjectivity revealed in both narratives. The impact of legal barriers, racial discrimination, and poverty that entangle Malian women is the dark underbelly of migrant life in France. Family life is especially undermined in ways very similar to the interlocking system of government assistance, housing, and social work that undermined African American family life in the nineteenth century. These texts give "voices to the voiceless" and once again, they demonstrate realistic, authentic, and finely sketched portraits of women's survival in the unwelcoming landscape of France.

Finally, critics of the new crop of fictional works produced by African authors and consumed in the West, interrogate the authenticity and conventional criterion for "African literature." In his "Presidential Address" at the 2018 African Literature Association conference Helon Habila forecasts "The Future of African Literature" and contextualizes recent trends in the fiction of contemporary African authors: "These writers, what I call 'post-national' writers, are daily showing us new potentials for African writing, what it can be when it is unfettered by tradition or national expectation" (158). Like other critics, he asserts the need for writers to continue moving beyond the concerns of the nation and to develop their creative artistry in new ways beyond conventional boundaries of postcolonial writing that began in the mid-twentieth century. The women writers in the collection are meeting this charge because Habila confirms the idea that "Our Africa has become these diasporic communities in which we live." (2019: 158). Thus, the fiction analyzed in the collection highlights the reimagined identities that emerge in diaspora spaces as well as new configurations of the relationship to Africa as homeland. African women are forging new frontiers in literature and in the process, creating a new aesthetic to foreground feminist energies, and shifting perceptions of the African *self* amidst new realities in transnational spaces. *African Women Writing Diaspora* (re)envisions a new landscape of creativity in an age of social, economic, and political transformation.

REFERENCES

Adichie, Chimamanda Ngozi. 2013. *Americana*. Toronto: Alfred A. Knopf.
Aidoo Ata, Ama. 1997. *Our Sister Killjoy Our Sister Killjoy: Or Reflections of a Black-Eyed Squint*. Lagos/New York: Nok Press.
Atta, Sefi. 2008. *Swallow*. Lagos: Farafina.
Atta, Sefi. 2010. *News from Home*. Northhampton: Interlink Books.
Boyce-Davies, Carol. 1994. "Migratory Subjectivities: Black Women's Writing and the Re-Negotiation of Identities." In *Black Women, Writing and Identity: Migrations of the Subject*, 1–37. London and New York: Routledge.
Dabiri, Emma. 2014. "Why I'm Not an Afropolitan"/Africa is a Country 1–11. https://africasacountry.com/2014/01/why-im-not-an-afropolitan/.2014.
Emecheta, Buchi. 1972. *In the Ditch*. London: Barrie and Jenkins.
Emecheta, Buchi. 1974. *Second Class Citizen*. New York: George Braziller.
Emecheta, Buchi. 1994. *Kehinde*. London: Heinemann.
Evaristo, Bernadine. 2020. *Girl, Woman, Other*. New York: Grove Press.
Eze, Chielozona. 2014. "Rethinking African Culture and Identity: The Afropolitan Model." *Journal of African Cultural Studies* 26: 234–247. http://dx.doi.org/10.1080/13696815.2014.894474.
Ezeigbo, Akachi Adimora. 2008. *Trafficked*. Lagos: Lantern Books.
Gehrmann, Susanne. 2016. "Cosmopolitanism with African Roots: Afropolitanism's Ambivalent Mobilities." *Journal of African Cultural Studies* 28(1): 61–72. http://dx.doi.org/10.1080/13696815.2015.1112770.
Gikandi, Simon. 2001. "Foreword on Afropolitanism." In *Negotiating Afropolitanism: Essays on Borders and Spaces in Contemporary African Literature and Folklore*, edited by Jennifer Wawrzinek and J. K. S. Makokha, 9–11. Amsterdam-New York: Ropodi.
Gikandi, Simon. 2011. "Foreword on Afropolitanism." In *Negotiating Afropolitanism: Essays on Borders and Spaces*, edited by Jennifer Wawrzinek and J. K. S. Makokha, 9–13. Amsterdam and New York: Rodopi.
Gyasi, Yaa. 2016. *Homegoing*. New York: Vintage Books.
Habila, Helon. 2019. "The Future of African Literature." *Journal of the African Literature Association* 13: 153–162.
Hasan, Salah M. 2010. "Rethinking Cosmopolitanism: Is 'Afropolitanism' the Answer?" http://www.princeclausfund.org/files/docs/5_PCF_Salah_Hassan_Reflections_120x190mm5DEC12_V.
Okorafor, Nnedi. 2010. *Who Fears Death*. New York: Daw/Penguin.
Okorafor, Nnedi. 2013. *What Sunny Saw in the Flames*. Abuja: Cassava Republic Press.
Roberts, Jennifer/The Globe and Mail. 2013. "New Novel Shows that Chimamanda Ngozi Adichie Gets the Race Thing." https://www.theglobeandmail.com/arts/boo

ks-and-media/new-novel-shows-that-chimamanda-ngozi-adichie-gets-the-race-thing/article12423909/.

Sackeyfio, Rose. 2014. "Black Women's Bodies in a Global Economy: Sex, Lies and Slavery in *Trafficked* by Akachi Adimora Ezeigbo and *On Black Sisters' Street* by Chika Unigwe." In *At the Crossroads, Readings of the Post-Colonial and Global in African Literature and the Visual Arts*, edited by Ghiramai Negash, 199–210. Trenton: Africa World Press.

Scego, Igiaba. 2015. *Adua: A Novel*. Translated by Jamie Richards. New York: New Vessel Press.

Selasie, Taiye. 2005. "ByeBye Babar." *The Lip Magazine*. http://thelip.robertsharp.co.uk/?p=76.

Tagoe, Nana-Wilson. 2009. "The African Novel and the Female Condition." In *The Cambridge Companion to the African Novel*, edited by Abiola Irele, 177–193. New York: Cambridge University Press.

Unigwe, Chika. 2009. *On Black Sisters' Street*. London: Jonathan Cape.

Unigwe, Chika. 2019. *Better Never Than Late*. Abuja-London: Cassava Shorts.

Wainina, Bingavyanga. 2016. "Interview by Wachira Kigotho." *Pan-Africans Versus Afropolitans-An Identity Crisis*. Africa Edition (University World News) Issue No. 172. http://www.universityworldnews.com/article.php?story=20160429165418809.

Wa Ngugi, Mukoma. 2013. "Things Come Together." *The World Today* 69(5) (October& November): 44–45.

Wa Ngugi, Mukoma. 2018. *The Rise of the African Novel: The Politics of Language, Identity and Ownership*. Ann Arbor: Michigan University Press.

Index

Abani, Chris, 3; *Becoming Abigail*, 10; *Virgin of the Flames*, 10
Aba Women's War of 1929, 98
Abiku, 67
Achebe, Chinua, 9, 68; *Things Fall Apart*, 2, 68
Acholonu, Catherine, 99
activism of women, 89–100. *See also* ecofeminism
Adesanmi, Pius, 39
Adichie, Chimamanda Ngozi, 9–10, 25–26, 122; *Americanah*, 9, 25, 73–85, 94, 105, 120–22; awards and distinctions, 9; *Half of a Yellow Sun*, 9; *Purple Hibiscus*, 9; *The Thing Around Your Neck*, 9; *We Should All be Feminists*, 9
Adimora, Akachi, 119
Adua (Scego), 120
Adulthood Rites (Butler), 103
aesthetics: affective, 79–80; literary, 76; transnational, 75–78
affective aesthetics, 79–80
African American, 16, 20, 25, 103; bildungsroman, 50; families and communities, 22; family life, 125; grandmothers, 22–23
African American Odyssey (Hines), 20

African and American: West Africans in Post-Civil Rights America (Halter and Showers-Johnson), 25
African bildungsroman, 49–50, 52
African literature, 1, 3, 9–11, 39, 83, 90, 117–20, 125
"The African Novel and the Feminine Condition" (Wilson-Tagoe), 123
African women: bodies, 18–19, 79–80; canonical male writing, 75; cultural misrepresentations, 74–76; Third World subject, 75, 80. *See also* women
"African Women, Resistance Cultures and Cultural Resistances" (Kuumba), 95
African Women's Union, 98
Afrofuturism, 7, 105–8, 110, 115
Afropessimism, 119
Afropolitan identity/lifestyles, 117–19
Afropolitanism, 118–20; Gikandi's interpretation, 119, 121–22; problem with, 120
Afuko-Addo, Nana, 16
Aidoo, Ama Ata, 3, 5; *Anowa*, 1, 5; *Changes*, 104–5; *Dilemma of a Ghost*, 1; *Our Sister Killjoy: Reflections of a Black-eyed Squint*, 3, 9, 10, 73–85, 90, 120, 121

Americanah (Adichie), 9, 25, 73–85, 94, 105, 120–22
Angelou, Maya, 23
Anowa (Aidoo), 1, 5
Anugwom, Edlyne, 95, 96, 98
Archer, O. Jermaine, 20
Arnett, James, 51
Asante people/culture, 16–18, 21–25
Asantewa, Yaa, 23–24
Atlantic Slave Trade, 5, 16
Atta, Sefi, 123–24; awards, 9, 90; *The Bead Collector*, 9, 90; *A Bit of Difference*, 9, 73–85, 89, 120–21, 124; *Everything Good Will Come*, 9, 90, 93; *News from Home*, 8–9, 89–100, 123; *Swallow*, 9, 90, 93, 124
Austen, Ralph, 48–49, 52
autobiography, 23
autodidactic learning, 52

Ba, Mariama, 1–2; *Scarlet Song*, 104; *So Long a Letter*, 2, 104
Baldwin, James, 125
The Bead Collector (Atta), 9, 90
Beautiful Things that Heaven Bears (Mengestu), 10
Becoming Abigail (Abani), 10
Behold the Dreamers (Mbue), 105, 120
Better Late than Never (Unigwe), 90, 120
Beyala, Calixthe, 32–37, 118; "*féminitude*", 33; *Loukoum: The Little Prince of Belleville*, 5, 6, 30, 32–37, 39–41, 125
Beyond the Horizon (Darko), 8, 59–63, 119, 122
Bhabha, Homi, 51
bildungsroman, 45, 46, 48–50; African, 49–50, 52; African American, 50; Austen on, 48–49, 52; European, 49, 52; feminist, 50; Moretti on, 48; postcolonial, 48, 50; Slaughter on, 46
Binti (Okorafor), 7, 107
A Bit of Difference (Atta), 9, 73–85, 89, 120–21, 124

black female body, 79–80; physical abuse, 19; violence against, 18–19
Black France: Colonialism, Immigration, and Transnationalism (Thomas), 32
black literary movement. *See négritude*
blackness, 25
"The Black Panther," 108
"Black Women's Bodies in a Global Economy: Sex, Lies and Slavery" (Sackeyfio), 8, 122
Black Women Writing and Identity (Davies), 117
blogging, 82–83
body. *See* black female body
Boni, Tanella, 30; *Que vivent les femmes d'Afrique*, 30
The Book of Phoenix (Okorafor), 107
"Born-to-Die" (McCabe), 67
Bracks, Lean'tin, 16, 22
Bulawayo, NoViolet, 7–8; *We Need New Names*, 7, 11, 45–56, 90–91, 124–25
Burnett, Joshua, 108
Busia, Abena P. A., 74
Butler, Octavia, 103, 105; *Adulthood Rites*, 103; *Dawn*, 103; *Imago*, 103; *Kindred*, 103; *Parable of the Sower*, 103; *Parable of the Talents*, 103
"Bye Abana Babar" (Selasie), 118, 120

Campbell, Emory S., 20
Campbell, Joseph, 106–7, 109, 112, 114; monomyth structure, 105–7; "separation-initiation-return" pattern, 106
Celles qui attendent (Diome), 41
Changes (Aidoo), 104–5
Charlie Hebdo, 31
Chevrier, Jacques, 32
"Citizens-in-Waiting, Deportees-in-Waiting: Power, Temporality, and Suffering in the U.S. Asylum System" (Haas), 54
civil society response, 98

civil war in Sudan, 65
Cole, Teju, 10
Conrad, Joseph, 78
Coulibaly, Amédy, 31
Country-Game, 52–53
Cros, Edmond, 61
cultural misrepresentations of African women, 74–76

Dabiri, Emma, 120
Dadié, Bernard, 29; *Un nègre à Paris (An African in Paris)*, 29
Danailova-Trainor, Gergana, 62
A Dance with Dragons (Martin), 107
Dangarembga, Tsitsi, 49; *Nervous Conditions*, 49–50, 52, 56, 105; *This Mournable Body*, 105
Darko, Amma, 8; *Beyond the Horizon*, 8, 59–63, 119, 122
A Daughter of Isis (Saddawi), 104
Davies, Carol Boyce, 27, 117
Dawn (Butler), 103
d' Eaubonne, Francois, 94
Diallo, Fatimata, 5, 6, 33–34; *Sous mon voile*, 5, 30, 32, 33, 37–41, 125
diaspora, 2–3; family patterns, 22–23. See also diaspora fiction
diaspora fiction, 1, 3–5; Francophone, 2, 5–6, 29–30, 40–41, 118, 125
Dilemma of a Ghost (Aidoo), 1
Diome, Fatou, 41; *Celles qui attendent*, 41
disenfranchisement, 97
disillusionment, 46, 47; postcolonial bildungsroman, 46, 48
Douceurs du bercail (Fall), 41
Douglass, Frederick, 19
Dugger, Celia W., 47
Duiker, K. Sello, 103
Dunbar, Michelle O.P., 64

ecofeminism, 94–100
economic mobility, 48
economic stagnation, 47–48
Ekine, Sokari, 95–96, 97, 99

Ekwensi, Cyprian, 2; *Jagua Nana*, 2
Emecheta, Buchi, 2–3, 90; *In the Ditch*, 2, 90, 121; *Kehinde*, 2, 121; *The New Tribe*, 2–3; *Second Class Citizen*, 2, 90, 104, 121
Emenyonu, Ernest, 3
environmental crisis, 8, 89–100. See also activism of women
Esty, Jed, 54
ethnic communities, 99
ethnic conflict, 65
ethnic hostility in France, 6
Etoké, Nathalie, 40
Europe, African immigration to, 40–41
European bildungsroman, 49, 52
Evaristo, Bernadine, 120; *Girl, Woman, Other*, 120
Everything Good Will Come (Atta), 9, 90, 93
Eze, Chielozona, 65, 66, 120
Ezeigbo, Akachi Adimora, 64

Fagunwa, D. O., 68
Fall, Aminata Sow, 41
family life, 125
The Famished Road (Okri), 103
Fanon, Frantz, 84
fantasy narratives, 104. See also magical realism
Felski, Rita, 50
"Female Power, Transformation and Re-imagined Futures in Nnedi Okorafor's *Lagoon*" (Sackeyfio), 124
female sexuality, 8
feminism, 32–33; hegemonic discourse, 74; transnational perspectives, 73–85
feminist bildungsroman, 50
féminitude, 33
Femme d'Afrique: la vie d'Aoua Kéita racontée par elle-même (Kéita), 29
Fofana, Aïcha, 33
Foreign Gods (Ndibe), 10
"Frames of Marginality: Emecheta's Legacy in the 21st Century" (Sackeyfio), 3

France: anti-natalist policies, 35–36;
  birthrate in, 35; immigration laws,
  33, 37; Le Pen family, 31; *Life
  Stories* project in, 33, 40; *migritude*
  literature, 32; *négritude*, 32; non-
  European immigrants, 35; Pasqua
  laws, 31; polygamy, 35; pro-natalist
  incentives, 35; sub-Saharan African
  population, 29; veil in, 38–39
Franco-Française, 36
Francophone diaspora fiction, 2, 5–6,
  29–30, 40–41, 118, 125
French National Assembly, 31
Front National (FN), 31
"The Future of African Literature"
  (Habila), 125

A Game of Thrones (Martin), 107
"The Game of Thrones," 107
gaze, 122–23; mobility and, 78–81
Gbaguidi, Célestine, 61
gender, 2, 5, 32–33, 41
Gender in African Women's Writing
  (Nfah-Abbenyi), 32–33
gender roles of Nigerian women, 93
German Third Reich, 83
Ghana, 15–27; Asante people/culture,
  16–18, 21–25; historical continuity,
  26; Queen Mother system, 24; slave
  trade, 5
Ghana Must Go (Selasie), 90
Gikandi, Simon, 119, 121–22
Girl, Woman, Other (Evaristo), 120
globalization, 59
Goyal, Yogita, 3, 52
grandmothers, 22–23
Greenbelt Movement in Kenya, 98
Grewal, Inderpal, 80
Gyasi, Yaa, 5, 91; awards, 5;
  Homegoing, 5, 11, 15–27, 91, 118,
  120, 123

Haas, Bridget, 54
Habila, Helon, 11, 125; "The Future of
  African Literature," 11, 125

Haley, Alex: *Roots: The Story of an
  American Family*, 20
Half of a Yellow Sun (Adichie), 9
Halter, Marilyn, 25
Hansberry, Lorraine, 23
Harlem Renaissance, 32
Harry Potter series (Rowling), 107–8
Hartmann, Ivor W., 6
Heart of Darkness (Conrad), 78
Henderson, Annie, 23
Hernandez, Diego, 62
The Hidden Star (Duiker), 103
hijab, 37
Hines, Darlene Clark, 20; *African
  American Odyssey*, 20
The Hobbits (Tolkien), 107
Hoeller, Hildegard, 78
Homegoing (Gyasi), 5, 11, 15–27, 91,
  118, 120, 123
Honwana, Alcinda, 47, 51, 54
human rights, 45–46
Human Rights Inc. (Slaughter), 46
human trafficking, 8, 10, 59–70;
  defined, 60; risks, 60. *See also* sex-
  trafficking
hybridity, 4, 11, 77–78, 90

identity, 1, 4, 10, 15; African, 2–3;
  hybrid, 7–8; politics, 25; racial,
  2, 4, 10; resistance and, 21–24;
  sexual, 10; speculative fiction and, 6;
  transnational, 1
ifá babaláwo, 67–68
Ikelegbe, Augustine, 98
I Know Why the Caged Bird Sings
  (Angelou), 23
Imago (Butler), 103
immigrant fiction. *See* diaspora fiction
immigration, 4, 5, 31, 39–41. *See also*
  Malian immigrants in France
Incidents in the Life of a Slave Girl
  (Jacob), 23
In the Ditch (Emecheta), 2, 90, 121
Irele, Abiola, 3
Isaacs, Camille, 51

Jacob, Harriet, 23
Jagua Nana (Ekwensi), 2
Jane Eyre, 52
Jeffrey, Craig, 47

Kehinde (Emecheta), 2, 121
Kéita, Aoua, 29; *Femme d'Afrique: la vie d'Aoua Kéita racontée par elle-même*, 29
Kelly, Liz, 61
Kester, Gunilla, 50
Kindred (Butler), 103
Kofman, Eleonore, 31
Krishnan, Madhu, 2
Kuoh-Moukoury, Thérèse, 29; *Rencontres essentielles* (*Essential Encounters*), 29
Kuumba, Bahati M., 95

Laczko, Frank, 62
Lagoon (Okorafor), 107
The Language You Cry In, 21
Lee, Yoon Sun, 4
Le Pen family, 31, 36
Lettre à la France Nègre ("Letter to Black France") (Ouologuem), 29
"Life in Zimbabwe: Wait for Useless Money" (Dugger), 47
The Life of a West Indian Slave (Prince), 19
lifespan of nationalist discourse, 50
Life Stories project in France, 33, 40
liminality, 55
liminal novel, 54–55
The Lion and the Jewel (Soyinka), 2
literary aesthetics, 76
literary representations of African female subjects, 74
literature: African, 1, 3, 9, 10–11, 39, 83, 90, 117–20, 125; as a cultural product, 11
Long JuJu Man (Okorafor), 7
The Lord of the Rings (Tolkien), 107
Loukoum: The Little Prince of Belleville (Beyala), 5, 6, 30, 32–37, 39–41, 125

Maggio, Jay, 74
magical realism, 68, 103–14; definition of, 104; monomyth, 105–7, 109–14; mythological universe, 104
Magical Realism and the Postcolonial Novel (Warnes), 104
Mali: polygamy in, 35; threat of terrorism in, 40
Malian immigrants in France, 5; adverse classifications, 30; *Loukoum: The Little Prince of Belleville* (Beyala), 5, 6, 30, 32–37, 39–41; marital status, 35; *Sous mon voile* (Diallo), 5, 30, 32, 33, 37–41
Mama Day (Naylor), 23
Mariage, on copie (Fofana), 33
Martin, George R. R., 107
Masquelier, Adeline, 47
Mbue, Imbolo, 105
McCabe, Douglas, 67
memory, 5, 16–27
Mende song, 21
Mengestu, Dinaw, 10; *Beautiful Things that Heaven Bears*, 10
migration, 4, 51, 89–90, 117, 123; forced, 59, 64, 65; globalization and, 59
Migrations of Identity (Davies), 27
migritude literature, 32
Mitterrand, François, 36
mobility, 76; gaze and, 78–81; sexuality and, 64–69; transcontinental, 77–78
Mobolade, Timothy, 67
Mohammed, Prophet, 31
Mohanty, Chandra Talpade, 74, 76, 79
monomyth, 105–7; *What Sunny Saw in the Flames* (Okorafor), 109–11; *Who Fears Death* (Okorafor), 111–14. See also magical realism
Moretti, Franco, 48
Motherism: The Afrocentric Alternative to Feminism (Acholonu), 99
Moudileno, Lydie, 5
Movement for Survival of Ogoni People (MOSOP), 98

Muponde, Robert, 50, 51
myths: defined, 104; origin stories, 104. *See also* magical realism

Naylor, Gloria, 23
Ndibe, Okey: *Foreign Gods*, 10
Ndlovu, Isaac, 51
Negotiating Afropolitanism: Essays on Borders and Spaces in Contemporary Literature and Folklore, 118
négritude, 32
Nervous Conditions (Dangarembga), 49–50, 52, 56, 105
News from Home (Atta), 8–9, 89–100, 123
The New Tribe (Emecheta), 2–3
"New Women's Writing: A Phenomenal Rise" (Emenyonu), 3
New York Times, 47
Nfah-Abbenyi, Juliana Makuchi, 32–33, 39, 40; *Gender in African Women's Writing*, 32–33
Nigeria: poverty, 65; unemployment, 65; women's activism, 89–100
Nwapa, Flora, 1; *Efuru*, 1, 2
Nyatetu-Waigwa, Wangari wa, 54–55

Odamtten, Vincent O., 81
Ogbanje, 67–68
Ògbójú Ọdẹ nínú Igbó Irúnmalẹ̀ (Fagunwa), 68
Ogoni people, 97–98
Ogundipe-Leslie, Molara, 75, 76
Ogunyemi, Chikwenye Okonjo, 68
oil, 95–98
Okonkwo, Christopher N., 67
Okorafor, Nnedi, 6, 7, 11, 103–5; awards, 7; *Binti*, 7, 107; *The Book of Phoenix*, 107; *Lagoon*, 107; *Long JuJu Man*, 7; *The Shadow Speaker*, 107; *What Sunny Saw in the Flames*, 6, 103, 106–11, 114, 124; *Who Fears Death*, 6, 7, 103, 106–8, 111–14, 124; *Zahrah the Windseeker*, 107
Okri, Ben, 103

Olaudah, Equiano, 16; *The Interesting Life of Olaudah Equiano*, 20
On Black Sisters' Street (Unigwe), 8, 11, 59, 64–69, 90, 105, 119, 122
Opala, Joseph, 21
Open City (Cole), 10
oppositional consciousness, 73; voicing and, 81–83
oppression, 73; comparative perspective on, 83–85; patriarchal, 2; transnational view of, 75
otherness, 90, 92
Ouologuem, Yambo, 29
Our Sister Killjoy: Reflections of a Black-eyed Squint (Aidoo), 3, 9, 10, 73–85, 90, 120, 121

The Palm-Wine Drinkard (Tutuola), 68
Parable of the Sower (Butler), 103
Parable of the Talents (Butler), 103
Pasqua laws of France, 31
"passage to Europe," 65
patriarchal oppression, 2
Peretz, Pauline, 33
The Phoenix (Unigwe), 105
physical abuse, 19
Pinto, Samantha, 76
polygamy, 35
postcolonial bildungsroman, 45, 46, 48–50, 56
postcolonial literature, 2, 3, 74
postcolonial predicament, 81
postcolonial subjectivity, 78
postcolonial writing, 46, 125
poverty, 96–97
Prince, Mary, 19; *The Life of a West Indian Slave*, 19
prostitution, 60
Purple Hibiscus (Adichie), 9
Putzi, Jennifer, 19

Quayson, Ato, 47
Queen Mother system, 24

Que vivent les femmes d'Afrique (Boni), 30
Quran, 38

"'Raising the Stigma': Black Womanhood and the Marked Black Body in Pauline Hopkins's *Contending Forces*" (Putzi), 19
A Raisin in the Sun (Hansberry), 23
Ransome-Kuti, Funmilayo, 98
Regan, Linda, 61
Rencontres essentielles (*Essential Encounters*) (Kuoh-Moukoury), 29
representational homogenization, 74
resiliency, sexuality and, 60–63
The Rise of the African Novel (Wa Ngugi), 11
Roots: The Saga of an American Family (Haley), 20
Rosanvallon, Pierre, 33–34
Rowling, J. K., 107–8
Rudolph, Alexandra, 62

Saddawi, Nawal El, 104
Salman, Aneel, 95
Saro Wiwa, Ken, 97, 98
Scarlet Song (Ba), 104
Scego, Igiaba, 120
science fiction (SciFi), 6
Second Class Citizen (Emecheta), 2, 90, 104, 121
Selasie, Taiye, 90, 118
"separation-initiation-return," 106
sex industry, 8
sex-trafficking, 60; *Beyond the Horizon* (Darko), 60–63; *On Black Sisters' Street* (Unigwe), 64–69
sexuality: mobility and, 64–69; resiliency and, 60–63
sex work, 60
sex workers, 8
The Shadow Speaker (Okorafor), 107
Shell oil, 98
Showers-Johnson, Violet, 25

Slaughter, Joseph, 45–46, 51; on bildungsroman, 46; *Human Rights Inc.*, 46
slave narratives, 19
slavery, 5, 62
slave trade, 5
social sciences, 4
So Long a Letter (Ba), 2, 104
Some Kinds of Childhood: Images of History and Resistance in Zimbabwean Literature (Muponde), 50
Sommers, Marc, 47; *Stuck: Rwandan Youth and the Struggle for Adulthood*, 47
The Song of Ice and Fire (Martin), 107
Sous mon voile (Diallo), 5, 30, 32, 33, 37–41, 125
Soyinka, Wole, 2; *The Lion and the Jewel*, 2
speculative fiction, 6, 107–8, 124
Spivak, Gayatri Chakravorty, 73, 74
"Struggling with the African Bildungsroman" (Austen), 48–49
Stuck: Rwandan Youth and the Struggle for Adulthood (Sommers), 47
subaltern representations, 74
Sudan, 65
Swallow (Atta), 9, 90, 93, 124

terrorism, 40
The Thing Around Your Neck (Adichie), 9
Things Fall Apart (Achebe), 2, 68
third space, 32
Third World women, 75, 80; visual representations of bodies, 80
This Mournable Body (Dangarembga), 105
Thomas, Dominic, 32
Tolkien, J. R. R., 107
Trafficked (Adimora), 119
Trafficked (Ezeigbo), 64
transnational aesthetics, 75–78

transnational feminism, 76–78
transnational identity, 1. *See also* identity
Tunca, Daria, 67
Turner, Lorenzo Dow, 20, 21
Tutuola, Amos, 68

Umezurike, Udechukwu Peter, 63
Un amour sans papiers (Etoké), 40
"Under my Veil." *See Sous mon voile* (Diallo)
Unigwe, Chika: awards, 8; *Better Late than Never*, 90, 120; *On Black Sisters' Street*, 8, 11, 59, 64–69, 90, 105, 119, 122; as leading African writers, 8; *The Phoenix*, 105
Universal Declaration of Human Rights (UDHR), 62
University of Paris, 34
Un nègre à Paris (*An African in Paris*) (Dadié), 29
Unseasonable Youth (Esty), 54

veil, 37–39
Villetanneuse, 34
Virgin of the Flames (Abani), 10
voicing and oppositional consciousness, 81–83

Wainina, Bingavanga, 122
waithood, 45–46; characteristics, 51; concept, 45, 47; economic stagnation and, 47–48; Honwana on, 47, 51, 54; as liminality, 55; as period of dynamic creativity, 47; temporalities, 54–55; terminology and usage, 46–47

Walking through Fire (Saddawi), 104
Wa Ngugi, Mukoma, 10–11, 125; *The Rise of the African Novel*, 11
Wardlow, Holly, 60
"War for the Golden Stool," 23
Warnes, Christopher, 104
wa Thiong'o, Ngugi, 103
The Way of the World: The Bildungsroman in European Culture (Moretti), 48
We Need New Names (Bulawayo), 7, 11, 45–56, 90–91, 124–25
We Should All be Feminists (Adichie), 9
Western media, 32
What Sunny Saw in the Flames (Okorafor), 6, 103, 106–11, 114, 124
Who Fears Death (Okorafor), 6, 7, 103, 106–8, 111–14, 124
Wilson-Tagoe, Nana, 123
Wizard of the Crow (wa Thiong'o), 103
women: activism, 89–100; African diaspora, 4; experiences, 1; Ghanaian, 15–27; Malian diaspora, 29–41
world literature, 9

Zahrah the Windseeker (Okorafor), 107
Zimbabwe, 7; economic crisis in, 47, 52; lifespan of nationalist discourse, 50; limited opportunities and migration, 54; Operation Murambatsvina, 47–48; postcolonial state, 52, 55
Zulfiqar, Sadia, 77

About the Contributors

Tomi Adeaga, PhD, teaches African literature at the Department of African Studies, Faculty of Philological and Cultural Studies of the University of Vienna, Austria. She co-edited *Payback and Other Stories – An Anthology of African and African Diaspora Short Stories* (2018). She is the author of *Translating and Publishing African Language(s) and Literature(s): Examples from Nigeria, Ghana and Germany (2006)*. She published a short story called "Marriage and Other Impediments" in African Love Stories; An Anthology (2006). She translated Olympe Bhêly – Quénum's *C'était à Tigony* into *As She Was Discovering Tigony* (2017). Her areas of interest include African literature studies, African diaspora studies, translation, and transnational studies.

Nancy Henaku holds a PhD in Rhetoric, Theory and Culture from Michigan Technological University and a master's degree in English from the University of Ghana. Her research examines the relations between rhetoric, subalternity, and power with an emphasis on the transnational dimensions of postcolonial contexts, including those related to transnational Afro-feminisms.

Amanda Lagji is Assistant Professor of English and World Literature at Pitzer College. She has appeared in *Safundi*, *Mobilities*, *ARIEL*, *Law, Culture & the Humanities*, *African Literature Today*, among others. Her book project, *Postcolonial Fiction and Colonial Time: Waiting for Now*, won the 2020 NeMLA Annual Book Award for best unpublished manuscript.

Elijah Adeoluwa Olusegun is a PhD student in the Department of English and Writing Studies, University of Western Ontario, Canada, where he is currently pursuing his doctoral studies on the writings of August Wilson. He is also an Assistant Lecturer in the Department of English, University of Lagos, Nigeria, where he teaches dramatic literature. His research interest covers such fields as postcolonial theory, literary theory and criticism, African literature, and American literature. He is a member of Canadian Association for Commonwealth Literature and Language Studies (CACLALS) and Modern Language Association (MLA).

Rose A. Sackeyfio is associate professor of English in the Department of Liberal Studies at Winston Salem State University. She completed a PhD at Ahmadu Bello University, Zaria, Nigeria, where she taught for 10 years. Her area of specialization and research interest is interdisciplinary and includes the literature of African and African diaspora women, women's studies, cultural studies, and recently, South Asian women's writing. Her publications and scholarly pursuits explore various aspects of the lives of African women in the global arena. Her publications include book chapters and peer-reviewed articles in the *Journal of the African Literature Association* and *African Literature Today.* She is the co-editor of a collection of critical essays, *Emerging Perspectives on Akachi Adimora Ezeigbo* (2017), a leading Nigerian writer. Presently, Dr Sackeyfio is writing a book of critical essays called *Other Spaces, Other Selves: New Landscapes of Identity in African Women's Writing.* Her current research project will investigate the experiences of African female students in China to examine mobility, identity, and belonging.

Cheryl Toman is currently the Chair of the Department of Modern Languages and Classics and Professor of French at The University of Alabama. Toman's research focuses on Francophone women writers from Cameroon, Gabon, and Mali. She is the author of two books, *Women Writers of Gabon: Literature and Herstory* (Lexington 2016) and *Contemporary Matriarchies in Cameroonian Francophone Literature* (Summa 2008). She also has published several edited collections, essays, and translations of African literature.